Blazing into the Creative Wilderness

Creativity and ADHD

by

James Phelps

Contents

Contents

For my wife, Debbie

She is always there, on the other side of the wilderness,

The treasure of my heart.

Author's Note

It was 2007 and I was tired of feeling like I was crazy. So I took a test...

During my school years teachers would tell my parents, "He has tremendous potential, but he just doesn't try."

I didn't try because I wasn't interested…unless I *was* interested. Know what I mean?

I did manage to graduate from high school and go on to college. I did better in college because I could choose what I wanted to take. I also played baseball. That helped.

During my career I've demonstrated flashes of brilliance. At times my creative output was phenomenal. But, when I had to do the drudge work…well, I flamed out. I developed a pattern of being in a job for a couple of years and then getting bored. I'd always do just enough…show flashes of potential, enough so they wouldn't fire me. But I'd soon quit.

I had a vague idea of what I wanted to do, but because I kept moving it was hard to find traction. Finally I went out on my own. Again, at times I was brilliant and kept my business cooking. Other times I would fall into boredom. While my work was always professional, it would take me longer to get through projects.

My relationships? Don't ask. Not good. Again, moments of connection and joy, and then the mire of day-to-day routines. Frankly, I've made a better boyfriend than a husband. I'm not proud of that, but it is what's so.

The older I became the more crazy I felt. I was getting fewer things accomplished. I'd go to the store and only remember a few of the things I went to buy. My mind would wander, and then I would hyper-focus, isolating myself in what had caught my interest. And there was more.

In 2008 I took Dr. Amen's online test. It suggested I might have ADHD. I didn't believe it. That was a condition kid's had, right? And I certainly wasn't a "Dennis-the-Menace" hyperactive kid.

But, things got worse, especially in my marriage. I sought a psychiatrist. I took an exhaustive test which included my wife answering the same questions about me, and I was diagnosed with Type II and V ADHD. My psychiatrist said that people with my ADHD tended to be creative types. He was right, because that's what I am. A Creative Type.

He put me on meds (which made me even nuttier, so I switched to a more natural approach) and suggested I also seek a therapist. I did. It took time, but I began to develop systems that would help me focus, get things done. Behaviorally I made simple progress – but, as most people with ADHD will attest, there was a lot of rubble from the damage I had done in my relationships.

I got to know myself intimately. My rhythms, what made me tick. What made me happy or kept me interested. What accountability meant. Thankfully, after accepting some essential truths about myself, committing to a course of change and implementing systems that made life less crazy, my marriage has finally become way less stressful and much happier.

The systems I implemented worked. Was I consistent with them? Not at first. But I started getting more done. I use those systems today. Am I consistent now? Not 100%, but they work and I keep moving forward.

You can, too.

This book is for adults with ADHD- and anyone interested in firing up their creative process. As an ADHDer, that's where you live. While I've heard tale of people with ADHD becoming professional organizers, accountants and other professions that seem to fly in the face of ADHD convention, most of the people with ADHD I've met have been highly creative in some way. That doesn't mean they were artists, writers, actors or involved in some other artistic pursuit (though many were). What they exhibited was a proclivity for creative, innovative thought, the ability to see things out of the ordinary. They have the ability to connect disparate things to find solutions, dream up new inventions, create new art – making connections most "normal" people typically wouldn't make.

You likely have those gifts, too. And, if you're like most, you aren't using them to your fullest.

That's why you need this book.

I've been a student of the creative process for over 25 years. If you can master the process, you can master ADHD. Believe it or not, the process is actually quite simple. It has form and flow. *Blazing into the Creative Wilderness* gets you in the flow.

Some of the principles presented here will be new, some may be familiar. The process, though, is universal. Don't short-shrift the process. Other than that, all I ask is that you keep an open mind and use what works for you.

Keep this one thing in mind as you read: you *are* a Creative Type. Be proud of this. Hold on to this. You are perfect as you are.

Introduction

This book is about being YOU – powerfully.

It is based upon the primary blessing that accompanies ADHD – you are innately creative and have capacities for much more in life than what you are currently experiencing.

If you have ADHD, chances are good that you have underachieved in school and your career; that you have experienced far more failure in your relationships and on-the-job than most; you have struggled with getting things done, being continually disorganized, and have been labeled "irresponsible" while you never achieve your potential. You have suffered from a lack of self-confidence and low self-esteem. You (and others) have a pretty low opinion of your prospects that anything will change.

Sound familiar?

But, what if I told you that you possess a secret weapon that will change the game? What if there was the possibility to transform your life from the stress of chaos and underachievement, to the power of generating life -affirming results that provide you with confidence, passion and success?

This secret weapon is something you were born with – it is the most powerful and life changing blessing associated with ADHD. You possess more creativity that 90% of the population. You are wired differently – and this can be a true advantage.

You see, adults with ADHD tend to be more creative than those who are "normal". That's what a University of Memphis study of undergraduate students concluded after testing them in 10 different measurable areas of creativity. The conclusion of the research was that adults with ADHD were better equipped to look at problems from multiple angles and conjure up numerous solutions and ideas.

This doesn't mean that every person with ADHD is a creative genius ready to take Madison Avenue by storm. In fact, a majority of ADHDers have difficulty during their careers and certainly in relationships. The ADHD brain fires differently. Without an understanding of how to harness your creativity and having a system in place, you can expect to produce the same results as you always have.

However, by mastering the process of living from your creative strengths you will no longer feel like you are a round peg trying to fit into a square hole. Instead of trying to become like everyone else (and stuffing your creative abilities), you will truly be YOU – and you will experience more productivity, balance, passion, purpose and peace.

In learning to master the creative process – and implementing the systems and practices introduced in this book – your life will be transformed (and, quite possibly, so will the lives of people around you).

This book is about giving voice to your brilliance. You may not believe in this gift now, but by absorbing the content of this book and doing the exercises, by the end you will be empowered to not only give voice to your thoughts and ideas, but put them into action consistently.

In Part One you have the opportunity to dive into *who you are*. In the Blazing Mind system we focus extensively on stories. More specifically, *your* stories.

Creativity, in large part, is a discovery of self. We write, paint, explore, start businesses, raise children and pursue dreams in service to society… and along the way forge an authentic identity. This involves a kind of storytelling that we live out moment by moment, day by day, year by year. It is your story – the most important story you will ever experience.

First, discover your historical roots. While you are a unique individual, you also carry with you a kind of genetic memory that's with you from the moment you are born. Discovering your roots can have a powerful effect. You learn about the risks taken by your ancestors, their trials and outcomes. And through them, you realize that what was in them is also within you.

And so, you live your story. The essential elements of story are driven by two powerful forces: passion and vision. These are also the essential elements required for creative output.

With *Blazing Mind Creativity*, passion is the product of interest and desire. What moves you? What insatiable curiosity do you harbor? What turns you on about life? What makes you happy? You know, what is that thing that, when you do it, you lose track of time when you're doing it? That's interest. True interest.

What are your strengths? Talents? Gifts? What do you do well? You'll identify the obvious ones – and discover new strengths that may have been hidden. Through the process of discovery you'll determine how well your talents match your interests. In the end, you'll have alignment – and the makings of a vision.

Once you've entered the realm of discovery, you'll thirst for knowledge. In Part Two you'll be introduced to the mechanics of the creative process. Time, environment, people, the ongoing acquisition of knowledge.

A famous advertising executive once said that creative brilliance begins with knowledge. It's axiomatic that the more interested you are in something, the more you learn about it. The more you learn, the more fired-up you are to dive deeper. At its most fundamental level, that's how the creative process works. How will you learn? Take classes, learn by doing, find a mentor? Through *Blazing Mind Creativity* you'll design a system for acquiring knowledge in a way that works for you long-term.

In any process time is also an essential element that must be considered. In the work world, time equals money. But, in the creative process, time equals focus. This is also true for those with ADHD. It is said that it takes those with ADHD twice as long to get things done as a "normal" person. However, in the creative world time isn't purely measured by ticks on the clock.
For the creative (and the ADHDer – synonymous?) time is about focus. What is the intensity level of your focus? How often do you focus on the things that move you? Are you losing track of time on the clock when you're doing it? This is how the creative type measures time.

And where do you do what you do? Environment is important. This includes place and people, Where do you work? Who is there with you and supporting you? Creativity isn't expressed in a vacuum.

The creative process is shaped like an hourglass. In Part Three you'll be immersed into the actual phases of the creative process. Like any discipline, there are essential functions that make a process work. Creativity is no different.

Generating ideas, initiating, maintaining focus, incubating, working through adversity and completing. These are the phases – and every creative endeavor will follow this path. Without exception.

Being knowledgeable of the process is vital. And, knowing where you are in the process actually provides you with confidence – especially during times of adversity.

When you begin a project everything seems rosy and bright. You may be filled with a palpable feeling of excitement that drives you forward. But, eventually you'll enter the wilderness, where adversity awaits, ready to pounce. In Part Four you'll be given a machete to cut through the various challenges you'll encounter.

You *will* encounter barriers. You *will* face challenges. And, if you're faithful to the process and understand the creative power you possess, you will fight through them all. At its core essence creativity is about solving problems – and the WWA system equips you with tools, resources and methods to overcome challenges and find solutions.

You'll learn that adversity is good. Challenges organically manufacture creative tension. This tension, if handled proactively, provides you with even more fuel and energy to keep moving forward.

Finally, there is completion. Part Five celebrates your accomplishment. But, completing isn't as easy as it sounds – especially for those with ADHD. One of the trademarks ADHDers share is stacks of unfinished projects. Sometimes this is okay – as you will discover as you engage the *Blazing Mind Creativity* system. But, to be truly considered creative, a project must come to completion.

Now, some "projects" like rearing children will take a lifetime. Others, like starting and running a business are long-term but have different completion phases, or provide a structure to complete many directed projects. And, of course, artistic pursuits like painting a picture or writing book have beginning, middle and end.

Throughout this book you will be provided exercises that will help you learn the *Blazing Mind Creativity* system. Do them at your own pace – but, *do* them. There's value in what you'll discover. I also suggest reading the book first, and then go back and do the exercises. After your initial read you'll have an idea where the system is taking you – you'll understand how doing an exercise in Part One relates to something in Part Four.

Entering the creative process is like wrestling with angels, especially for ADHDers. The creative gifts and talents you've been given are exciting. There is a purpose behind your vision. You have the feeling you're doing something important. But, you must work for it. Creativity is sometimes messy and never easy. It's what makes you human. How you give life to your creativity is what makes you, *you.*

That's what makes the struggle so sweet. Because when you wrestle with angels you will always be given a gift. It may cost you something…but you'll always receive a blessing.

That blessing is always worth the cost.

Part One: Identity

Are You Who You Think You Are?

"Identity is such a crucial affair that one shouldn't rush into it."
---David Quammen

"Live your eyeliner, breathe your lipstick..."
——Lady Gaga

"All discomfort comes from suppressing your true identity"
---Bryant H. McGill

"I am the Lizard King."
---Jim Morrison

Who are you?

Why Creativity and ADHD?

"The only problem with the world is a lot of people DON'T have ADD!"
   ---Andy Pakula, CEO of Think! Interactive Marketing

I was diagnosed with ADHD in 2007. At the time I was shocked, angry, relieved and, strangely, comforted, all at once. The older I became, the more miserable the manifestations of ADHD had made my life.

The diagnosis made me angry because I immediately went into victim mode, "Why me?" Why did God curse me with this neurological disorder? Looking back I could see how it had affected my life - and I wasn't happy. I also wasn't happy that I wasn't diagnosed earlier. Wouldn't the track of my life have gone better if I had been diagnosed and treated?

But, the ADHD diagnosis is fairly new as disorders go. And, within a short time I accepted my condition and actually experienced relief. I wasn't crazy. There was an explanation for why I did the things I did. I devoured information about the disorder quickly and came to an understanding of why I did the things I did, and how this behavior could be managed. While I still must battle through many aspects of the disorder on a daily basis, it no longer limits me.

Finally, I embraced the disorder. My psychiatrist told me that the variety of ADHD I possessed was shared by many creative people he treated: artists, poets, writers. This comforted me.
Having always been a creative type, I took great interest in learning how the creative process worked. I read everything I could get my hands on about the psychology of creativity. I talked to fellow artists, writers, entrepreneurs and others whom I considered to be creative.

And so, when I was diagnosed with ADHD, and hearing what my psychiatrist said, I began doing the work to make the connections as to not only "why", but "how".

First, the study of creativity is relatively new. There have been a few researchers who have devoted their lives to the subject - and I've studied their work. Second, many creative types have written about creativity from a more poetic and less research-oriented perspective. All of this has been useful. But, there has been little or no useful information about the connection between creativity and ADHD - until now.

Professors Holly White and Priti Shah studied 60 Memphis University undergrads, half of whom had ADHD. They discovered that, yes, those with ADHD scored much higher in the areas of "divergent" thinking than those who did not have ADHD. Divergent thinking is the ability to generate spontaneous ideas and/or solutions, many of which seem to come from left field. Divergent thinkers tend to take more risks, seek originality and are more comfortable with ambiguity. Convergent thinkers (opposite of divergent) are often more linear, organized and focused.

While I do not want to get into all of the particulars of the study (after all, it was only 60 college kids), one of the trends the researchers found was that those with ADHD scored much higher in those areas of creativity in which inhibitions are shed. For example, the students with ADHD did better in creative areas like drama and performance than those without ADHD.

Given the "hyperactivity" part of ADHD, this makes a lot of sense, doesn't it? But, it also underscores one of the basic problems in diagnosing ADHD in children.

Boys are three-times more likely to be diagnosed with ADHD as children than are girls. Why? Because boys tend to exhibit the lack of inhibition in a more in-your-face manner. Girls, on the other hand, tend to exhibit more of the passive traits. While things are beginning to change as we understand more about this disorder, this gives us a clue as to why more and more adult women are being diagnosed with ADHD.

Coming full circle, I want to encourage people with ADHD - whether diagnosed as a child or as an adult - that this "disorder", if handled the right way, is a blessing and not a curse. That, in fact, you were made perfectly by a perfect Creator.

While I contend that all human beings are Creative Types - those of us with ADHD were specially wired to be creative. There's a reason that we excel at divergent thinking, and that we do better with shedding inhibitions - we must!

One of the things I really enjoy is public speaking. Several years ago an Ivy League school did a survey on what people were most afraid of - and public speaking trumped dying as a source of fear! With that evidence in hand, why are there crazy people like me who actually enjoy getting in front of people and talking?

Simple. It's the dopamine hit.

I get just as nervous before giving a talk as anyone else. While I think I do a pretty good job at speaking, there are many many many more who are better at it than me. But, once I get off the stage, I'm buzzing, excited, ready for more. Others might be just glad their time at the podium is over and done, but not me...I want more. I like the neurochemical hit that comes with speaking in front of strangers.

The creative process is a journey into the unknown. That's exciting. ADHD brains thrive on excitement. Our brains are wired to produce excitement - because our neurology needs the chemical infusion to feel "normal". That's why drugs like Ritalin and Aderrall are prescribed - they are amphetamines. They simulate and stimulate.

But, nothing can take the place of the real thing. The problem is, we can't get enough of the real thing. That's why so many children are hyperactive, and so many adult ADHDers are depressed. Kids can go and go and go. As adults, we have our place in life and deviation from that place isn't accepted. Uninhibited behavior is expected of us as children, frowned upon as adults.

That's why for adults with ADHD, creativity is the best drug. Ordering your life in such a way that you can participate in creative activity daily is important. In fact, I think for ADHDers, being creative is the essence of being alive. God gave us the hardware to create, innovate and produce in ways that "normal" people do not have. The "normies" out there must work much harder at creative pursuits - whereas it comes more naturally for those with ADHD.

That being said, creativity does have a process - and people with ADHD are not as well suited for linear procedures that require high levels of organization and redundant activity. While studies have shown that there is little difference between those with and without ADHD with regards to implementing skills, people with ADHD do have challenges with follow-through, finishing and remaining focused on singular tasks.

For this reason Creative Types must learn, understand and master the actual creative process. *Blazing into the Creative Wilderness* provides this guide with practical tips and an honest assessment of what we're up against.

Research is terrific. It validates much of what we've lived through. But, there is no greater teacher than life experience. Unlike our "normal" brothers and sisters, we must master another layer of skills if we are to truly be successful. Mastering the creative process is what we must do.

When we do this, we begin to truly fulfill our true nature.

Our True Nature

"So God created man in his own image, in the image of God he created him; male and female he created them."
---Genesis 1:27

This is my theory:

When God reached into the dust and formed man in His own image, He did so in detail. As the all-seeing-knowing-ever present Creator of the Universe who exists inside and outside of time, He knew sin would enter the world.

For that reason, He gave us two important gifts: Free Will and Creativity. Neither can exist without the other. Having the freedom to choose enables us to make all kinds of decisions, many of them being bad. And bad decisions –which could be sinful (i.e. missing the mark) - naturally lead to problems.

Thankfully, the Creator gave us a tool to solve these problems – creativity. Human beings are the only species on Earth that possesses this unique ability. A blend of reason, imagination, visioning, analysis, communication and invention, it involves a faculty for thinking, planning and taking action. It is a *process*. This problem-solving process can lead to the creation of something completely new, though more often we innovate – which is the act of improving on something that already exists.

Either way, we are acting out our true nature. Made in His image, we, too, are creators.

Especially those of us blessed with ADHD. Our brains really do fire differently. It is possible for us to hold many possible solutions in our mind all at once. We can imagine multiple futures. The ideas come fast, too. So fast sometimes others can't keep up. For those with ADHD, this process is like breathing.

So, whenever we deny our creative selves, whether it's from laziness, apathy, or the misguided belief that you think you're not creative, we are denying the critical attribute that makes us human.

We're all Creative-Types.

Society gets weird about creative-types. Assigning them to a certain social niche, when we think "creative-type" we often think of artists, musicians, designers, writers, inventors, advertising executives, journalists and sometimes accountants. Most in society call us weird.

Sadly, these days we also cut-off creative development in our children by the time they reach high school as administrators and politicians eliminate funding for art and music programs. We've left creativity in childhood. And, we often ascribe childish characteristics to adult creative-types – free spirits, irresponsible, flaky, unreliable, and undisciplined. These are also many of the qualities associated with having unmanaged ADHD.

Yes, Creatives *can* be those things, but many are not. For those that *are* those things…well, they make life more interesting, don't they?

People are people. Everyone has faults, character defects and weaknesses. We also have strengths, expertise (in something), and natural abilities. The potential for genius is in everyone.

We're all Creative Types. We can't help it. It's our nature. If you were born with ADHD, you were perfectly made. Yes, you are truly perfect as you are.

Blazing Into the Creative Wilderness is about how to harness your own creative strength and power. The more knowledge you gain and the more you engage the process, the greater your level of happiness, contentment and fulfillment will be. The more you will contribute.

It's also helpful to understand how this thing called creativity works. And so, there are five types of Creatives.

The 5 Creative Types

Know thyself, says the Oracle…

Self-reflection and introspection is always a good thing in small doses. Too much and analysis paralysis sets in. Too little and we can find ourselves way off course. Sometimes when the winds of change blow, we find our true direction.

In knowing ourselves, it's helpful to understand what "type" of creative we are.

We all have natural strengths. Understanding our strengths provides insight into the type of creative we are (keeping in mind that we have full access toward being each type of creative). Yes, this is shameless typecasting. And, yes, being type-cast can really suck. But, sometimes we just gotta know where to start. The good news is that during our creative life we will weave in and out of each type.

The Genius.
Some believe we all possess genius. We probably do. But, there are some who simply *are*. Mozart, Einstein and DaVinci come to mind (and many believe that each of these men had ADHD). The genius is a little odd,

different. They go their own way, sometimes to the detriment of their families and friends. They live "in their own world" - and eventually change the world in some way.

Typically the Genius is focused on a single domain like physics or music, and they spend a lifetime plunging deeper into their field. Different fields have different qualities. For example, most math and music geniuses have their most productive times during their 20's and 30's, while many painters don't reach full expression until much later in life. Here's the thing though: while we all possess a little genius, and there are very few actual full-blown geniuses roaming the earth.

First, most people want a balanced life filled with an integration of work, family, friends and an occasional vacation. The Genius tends to eschew these things -or marginalizes them - in favor of seeking answers to their creative problems with a religious fervor and myopic focus. Their work is all consuming and balance is a fairy tale.

Second, the Genius is in full acceptance and knowledge of their natural abilities. Like a 13-year old who discovers he can hit 35-foot jump shots with ease, they get in touch with their natural abilities early in life. They will tend to focus on these abilities to the *exclusion* of being well-rounded - and even have difficulty in school (like Einstein) due to bore-dom or stubbornness. With this early acceptance, they dive into their sub-ject with complete abandon - and that's how they become geniuses. (Disclaimer: of course it is entirely possible that a genius can certainly be well-rounded and have a depth and breadth of knowledge in multiple ar-eas. They can also have very deeply connected and loving relationships, too,)

Finally, fear often keeps mere mortals from becoming this kind of gen-ius. They want a "normal" life so they trade their exclusive genius for balance or promotions or time with family and friends. The Genius may feel out of place at times in the world, but they aren't really in this world – they are in *their* world.

While the Genius is kind of like the mad uncle who spends day and night in his workshop, we need them. They have the ability to pull disparate pieces of knowledge or inspiration seemingly from nowhere and create fabulous inventions, philosophies and art that propel the culture forward.

The Master Innovator.
The Master Innovator is more practical and typically is found in the realms of business, finance and government. They take existing ideas and make them better, more usable, more profitable, more efficient, etc. Bill Gates comes to mind. He took the basics of computing and, rather than being focused on the hardware, took existing software and made it easier to use. Windows is an excellent example of this. After all, point-and-click was an Apple-thing (and, before it was an Apple-thing, it was a Xerox-thing). Microsoft took that idea and created an operating system that changed the computing marketplace forever.

 Just like the Genius, the Master Innovator works every bit as hard at her craft and in her domain. But, there are external factors to be considered. The Genius is concerned with *"can this be done?"* The Master Innovator says, *"Okay, it can be done. How can it be done better?"*

While the creative process is the same, the Master Innovator isn't as concerned with originality as he is with functionality. Externalized forces – market opportunities, customer satisfaction, contributing knowledge – formulate the creative tension necessary to propel innovation. The Genius pushes the boundaries of natural law. Master Innovators push the limits of economies. Sometimes it works fabulously well (e.g. Microsoft Windows or the Toyota Prius), and sometimes it creates disaster (e.g. Adjustable Rate Mortgages). Either way, the Master Innovator has been responsible for propelling quality of life forward, versus changing the foundation of culture.

The Practical Creative.
This is where most people live. In our day-to-day lives we each find ways to make life easier and more livable. The Practical Creative focuses on the finer details. Kind of like the 3M guy who used a throw-away formula for a super glue to create sticky notes for his choir hymnal (and then the Master Innovator came along and took that idea and applied it to office stationary, creating a billion-dollar product line). Sometimes the practical ideas to make life better explode into the consciousness of entire populations.

Most of the time it's just personal stuff, like discovering that, while fishing, largemouth bass like the taste of peanut butter. As creativity researcher Mihalyi Csikzentmihalyi describes, it is flashes of brilliance.

I have a friend who lives on 16-acres of ranch land. To break the boredom, his 17-year old son fashioned a nine-hole golf course, using rocks, trees and other natural elements of landscape as boundaries for his "course". It required vision, innovation and imagination. While he had to bend and change the traditional rules of golf a little, it worked – and he and his dad have had a wonderful time playing his course (and avoiding rattlesnakes near the 7th "green").

The secret to Practical Creativity is to give yourself permission to not only think out of the box, but to sometimes remove the box altogether. Getting yourself out of the rut of routines is the trick. That's not so easy sometimes. A great way to break the routine addiction is, for 15-30 minutes a day, to focus on a specific problem in any area of life – work, relationships, parenting, etc – and allow your mind to roam, coming up with as many ways to solve the problem. The key is to eliminate your internal editor during this time. Once done, you might find a way to do something differently that will make a difference in your life and the lives of those around you. That's Practical Creativity.

The Closet Creative
You know who you are. The Closet Creative writes her novel when everyone has gone. She doesn't want others – especially family members – to know she's writing it. She's afraid they'll tell her it's a waste of time.

It's the guy who'll sing along with Andea Bocelli while driving, but won't open his mouth during worship at church. He's afraid someone will hear him.

Unfortunately, to a certain extent we are all Closet Creatives. Most people have a secret desire to sing, dance, write, paint, trade stocks, crochet, build houses…you get the picture. But, because they fear criticism or have no self-confidence, they never invest themselves publicly. However, they can't help but dream of writing that novel. So, they wait until they are alone and write.

It's the story line from the movie *Shall We Dance?* Richard Gere is an estate attorney who rides a train from Chicago to his home in the suburbs daily. And every day he passes a dance studio. Through the lit window he sees people learning how to dance. He also sees the elegant form of Jennifer Lopez. One evening he doesn't go home – and visits the dance studio instead. From there he begins his alternate life as a dancer. He never tells his wife. When he's finally found out he explains that he's embarrassed. They have so much, and yet he was dissatisfied with his life. Passing by the dance studio triggered something deep within him. It wasn't that he didn't love his wife and daughter. He did. There was just something missing.

The Closet Creative passes by dance studios dreaming of being the next Ginger Rogers or Fred Astaire. One day the resistance snaps. They just can't let the urge pass them by. But, until then, they may not feel like their environment is safe enough to venture out. And that's sad.

The Untapped Creative
This is the person who just doesn't know. Somewhere out there a person as brilliant as Einstein exists, but, he's working a backhoe in Nebraska. Or, maybe there's a future CEO for an amazing start-up making pizzas in New Jersey.

So few of us realize our true potential or understand and develop our innate strengths, talents and abilities. If we did, how much happier would we all be? Especially those who feel trapped in what they are doing – be it a personal relationship, job, industry or environment.

I think every kid during their sophomore year in high school should be tested for their innate strengths. Forget SAT's and all this inane standardized testing. *Find out who these kids really are!* Once their true strengths are identified, support them in developing their full potential. All too often we focus on a kid's weakness. And then that follows them during adulthood.

There are people with ADHD who have become professional organizers. Does that make sense? People with ADHD are the most *dis-organized* people in the universe, right? The thing is, we just see organization differently. These Creative Types have a gift for abstract organization that really works for them and the people they help. And they are passionate about what they do! But, in high school their desks and lockers may have been utter chaos. The well-meaning school counselors may have taken one look and told them they better learn how to operate heavy equipment or learn to sell cars.

It's the content, not the cover. Maybe if children and high schoolers were given tests to determine their creative aptitudes, perhaps ADHDers would score off the chart!

Which Creative Type are you? If you manage people, what Types are they? How about family and friends? Who are they? My guess is that we each possess traits from each type. We each have a unique genius that simply needs to be set free.

Stories.

Scallywags, Quaker Pirates and War Heroes:
The Making of the Family Brand

"Do not remove the ancient landmark that your ancestors set-up"
---Proverbs 22:28

(Note: This chapter is about family stories. You may ask, "What does this have to do with anything?" Well, I'll tell you. People with ADHD have tendencies toward low self-esteem. It is believed that ADHD is heredi-tary. When we connect to heroes from our family line, it can provide hope and a belief that we, like our ancestors, can achieve wonderful, and sometimes rebellious, feats.)

My brother, Tom, joined The DNA Project a few years ago. By supply-ing a sample of his DNA, he tapped into a biology-based ancestral track-ing project. Legal records, old photos, letters and stories passed down provide context, but because it is biology-based, the ancestral record is more reliable than by just relying on traditional means of tracking the family line.

It's revealed some interesting details about our clan.

Nearly two centuries ago I had a couple of cousins, a brother and sister, in Pennsylvania who got bored with their sedate Quaker lifestyle. They stole away during a warm summer night and escaped to South Carolina, where they set up shop as merchants with a very exclusive clientele: Blackbeard. Apparently they acted as the infamous pirate's "fence" for the property he acquired on the high seas. It's rumored that the cousins occasionally joined Blackbeard's crew. They had the family *Scallywag* Gene.

I also had an uncle who was a riverboat gambler on the Mississippi. One night he won half the state of Oklahoma when he laid down Kings over tens. The next night, of course, he lost it back when three Aces beat his two-pair. *Scallywag.*

And there was my uncle Shorty (who was over 6-feet tall – just for the record).

His platoon was in the Philippines during the War in the Pacific. In fact, he was there when McArthur made his triumphant entry. Long before that, though, his platoon was engaged in a fierce fire-fight with the Japanese. The American forces had taken a hill in a strategic location and were defending it throughout the night. Shorty said that his machine-gun barrel pulsed red from the heat of the constant firing into the dark. Because the fighting was so intense, and the battle took place during the blackness of night, he wasn't aware of what went on around him with his brothers. He just fired his gun. The fighting subsided as dawn broke. His brothers to the left and to the right were dead – as was ¾ of his platoon. When he went to wipe the grit from his brow, Shorty discovered that an enemy bullet had pierced his helmet just an inch above the top of his head. The cost was terrible, but they held the hill. Shorty was given ample accolades for his bravery – though he would rarely speak of his time in the Pacific.

Of course, Shorty, too, possessed the *Scallywag* Gene. Soon after the Japanese had surrendered, Shorty was busted down from sergeant to private because he smacked an officer in the mouth.

My contention that these, and many others in our clan, had ADHD – which could also be called the *Scallywag Gene*.

Knowing who you are is essential (especially the rascally part – I'm convinced that to be a true Creative, there needs to be a little bit of Scallywag in you). Family stories will give you a clue. While you are *not* your ancestors, and you are *not* a helpless victim to the historical record, I believe there *are* genetic dispositions that are a part of your make-up. And there is evidence that ADHD can certainly run in families.

Several years ago I had a job that required me to commute over an hour one-way. During the summertime I would occasionally take my daughter with me. At that time she was 8 or 9 years old. To keep her from getting bored (and save me from listening to the Back Street Boys or some other boy band), I began telling her stories. These were family tales passed along to me from my grandmother, Ila.

She was an all-time great storyteller.

In addition to the tales of Shorty and our card-playing uncle, I explained to Shannon how three brothers stole a boat in Dublin Harbor and sailed across the Atlantic into New York (*Scallywags*? You bet!). Because of the horrible way the Irish were treated in New York, two of the brothers moved toward the Great Lakes and started a cobbler business – Kinney Shoes. The other brother, my great-great grandfather, moved south. He would later take part in the Oklahoma Land Run in 1889.

She also learned of her creative link through the family connection to Lotta Crabtree, the Belle of the Barbary Coast. An actress, singer and dancer, her career was managed by her mother, Mary Ann. A proper English lady, Mary Ann wanted Lotta to join a prestigious ladies' club in Breslin Park, New Jersey (where Mary Ann owned a 22-room summer cottage). But, because Lotta smoked a trademark black cigar – no doubt a habit picked up while playing in the rough and tumble opera houses of Gold Rush California – she was never asked to join. The *Scallywag* Gene was alive and well in Lotta Crabtree!

This ritual of telling her stories became a connection point for us as father and daughter. She developed an insatiable appetite for the stories that brought our history to life. Though perhaps not a major factor in her development, now at 21 my daughter is a wonderful artist and full-fledged Creative Type (like Lotta – and her Dad!). In fact, connecting with her Irish roots, she chose as her Senior Project in high school to learn to speak Gaelic. She's gone on to study art history and film in college.

Shannon can now recite the family stories. They've been transformed, no longer just being *my* stories…but becoming *her* stories, as well. This is her family…her *brand*, so to speak. A part of her identity will come from these tales. Providing a kind of richly textured backdrop, they are a brilliant reminder of where she has come from, to what she is connected and rooted to. No matter what happens in her life, she will always have our stories to lean upon.

Thus, stories create the tapestries of life. Since the dawn of human history we have told stories. Our collective history is written on cave walls, stone tablets, and papyrus scrolls. They are illuminated in ancient manuscripts, bound between leather covers. They are contained in handwritten letters, recorded by printing presses, captured on silent 8mm film, stored on videotape, and can be seen on U-Tube. They are inscribed into our DNA. The author Ursula LeGuin said, *"Not every society used the wheel, but every society told stories."*

Storytelling is a part of us. All of the great teachers throughout history have told stories. From Homer to Jesus of Nazareth to Martin Luther King, we have been cultivated, molded and led by those who could spin compelling, value-laden tales…stories that moved us to take action. These stories changed us and altered the culture around us.

I firmly believe that our stories provide an essential *context* for our individual and collective creative process. After all, the human brain *thinks* in stories. When new information is introduced, the mind processes this information in the form of metaphors – the brain needs a story to make the information relevant. It is estimated that the human mind processes up to seven metaphors per minute.

Knowing your family's treasured stories is a vital link to your own creative nature. They can help you when you're in need. For example, when Shannon needs a shot of courage, she can resurrect Shorty defending the hill. If she needs a little pluck and fire, she can imagine Lotta puffing on her little black cigars. If she's hesitant about taking a risk, she can conjure the tale of our Quaker Pirate ancestors. Like all of us, she has the *Scallywag* Gene, It's there for her to tap whenever it's needed.

The thing is, the stories become archetypes for us. They are tools to guide us, inspire us, and connect us to a collective historical life that is larger than our own. And yet, your unique individual story is an essential component of this historical/genetic record.

The one persistent truth in all of this is that each of us has a story to tell.

And it's worth telling.

Our 4 Lives

"Human labor, through all its forms, from the sharpening of a stake to the construction of a city or an epic, is one immense illustration of the compensation of the universe. The absolute balance of Give and Take, the doctrine that everything has its price: if that price is not paid, not that thing but something else is obtained."
---Ralph Waldo Emerson, from *Essay III: Compensation*

One of the most memorable lines from the movie *The Natural* comes from Iris, Roy Hobbs' childhood sweetheart.

Discovered at a local fair in which he struck out *The Whammer* (a Babe Ruthian character), Hobbs was signed to a minor-league contract and left the farm when he was in his late-teens, early-20's. After a roll in the hay with Iris, he boarded a train and left to make his mark in the game he loved.

However…aboard the train he met a mysterious veiled woman, Harriet Bird, who captured his fancy. After telling her that his goal was "to be the best there ever was", Harriet pulled a Derringer from her handbag and shot poor Roy in the gut – and then made her own exit from the world of the living through an open third story window. For Roy, the bullet in the gut brought his Big League dreams to a crashing halt – for now.

Fast forward 20 years – Roy has been signed to play for the pitiful New York Knights. There is a power struggle going on between Pop, part owner and field manager of the club, and The Judge – Pop's corrupt partner. If the Knights don't win it all, Pop loses control of the team to The Judge. And, for that reason, The Judge has his field scouts signing players who can't possibly help Pop and the Knights win. And so, they sign the middle-aged Roy Hobbs.

Of course, Roy goes on to become a middle-aged rookie phenom, hitting homeruns by the bunch and leading the Knights to play winning ball. That is, until he falls for the beautiful Memo Paris – the blonde vixen assigned to seduce Roy by a gambler, and take his focus away from the game.

It works. He goes into a terrible slump at the plate.

One bright day in Chicago, as Roy is standing in the on-deck circle, he feels a presence. He doesn't know what it is or where it's coming from – it's just there. Then, up to bat, he swings and misses badly on the first two pitches. In the stands, a grown Iris stands up, a golden halo of sunlight shrouding her. Roy sees her, but his focus is on the next pitch – which he launches into the large clock 50 feet above the center field fence.

After the game he and Iris connect. He goes to visit her at her home. She asks, "What happened to you?"

He answers, "Life didn't turn out the way I thought it would."

Iris, her own bit of golden Yoda-mystery wisdom going on says, "You know, I think we have two lives: the one we learn with, and the one we live with." And then they move on to a less painful subject...

As much as I love that interaction (and that movie), Iris was only halfway there. I actually think we have *four* distinct lives. And, understanding these four lives is important if one is to dive head-long into the creative process. They are:

The Life We Could Have Had. Look back at your life. There are bound to be a number of key decisions you made that set your course. You are where you are now because of the decisions you made back then. Had you made different choices during those times, your life would be different today (probably). For example, what if you turned down your husband's marriage proposal and married someone else, or even went off to Paris to paint in the City of Light? What if you accepted that job halfway across the country? These big decisions mark us and follow because they can never be undone. When you look back, do you have any regrets? Many? A few? Maybe there's nothing you would change. No matter what course you chose, these decisions have led to the second life...

The Life You Learn With. The intimation from Iris is that this life is the one marked by mistakes, wrong turns, taking up with the wrong woman or man, overcoming challenges, winning, losing, and any other event that moulds character – experience that forms our historical life tapestry. Hopefully we learn from these experiences and make more informed and powerful decisions in the future. While we do learn something from our successes, it is from our failures that the real life value comes. Pain, disappointment and anger are all masterful teachers. The question is, will we pay attention to the lessons? Artistry of any kind is built upon failures. Some are small and seemingly inconsequential. Others are whoppers – colossal failures that, at the time, seem like the apocalypse and the dropping of the A-Bomb all in one shot. We are devastated, believing we can never recover.

But, we usually do – and we become much smarter for having the experience. This is the road to Mastery – and pain is always a companion and teacher. Of course, these lessons form the life with which we have the most familiarity…

The Life We Live With. There are consequences and rewards that accompany every decision we make. Nothing in life goes without compensation. Emerson's great essay that forms the Law of Compensation is dead-on. To the degree we're willing to pay the price is the degree to which we will have what we want.

For example, if you have a dream of being a professional baseball player, there is a price to be paid. Assuming you have a little bit of talent for the game, are you willing to work hard? Run five miles a day? Hit the weight room four days a week? Take batting practice until your hands bleed? Field 500 ground balls, catch 500 fly balls in the outfield, or train your body for years to increase the velocity of your fastball by just 2 miles per hour? And then…if you are the one in a million who is actually signed to play professionally, are you willing to take the long bus rides from town to town in the minor leagues? Perhaps for years?

I have a friend who played ball in the Minnesota Twins chain. He made it as far as AA. After a mediocre season in Orlando, he was released. Not wanting to give up his Major League dreams, he played in the Mexican League for a year. He recalls taking 18-hour bus rides with no air conditioning during the middle of a Mexican summer (with a complimentary keg of *Dos Equis* in the back of the bus); playing in ramshackle ballparks (in one town, a railroad track went through the outfield. The game was put on-hold at 8:15 each night as the train came through). He lasted a year, and then called it quits. Today he's a college baseball coach.

Emerson's Law of Compensation says that to obtain that which is desired, one must "pay every penny." My friend was willing to pay much, but not all, to become a Major League ballplayer. Since the "dream outcome" is never guaranteed – even if every penny is paid – we need to know ourselves, our environment, and our domain thoroughly in order to make powerful and empowering assessments. My friend possessed this knowledge and determined that he'd taken the Major League dream as far as he wanted to take it.

While that dream came to an end, a new one took over as a coach. Because he has professional baseball experience, it is quite possible that the Major League dream could be manifested by being a coach in the big leagues. Dreams don't have to die – they may need to be transformed.

He's content in this transformed life. It's brought about new goals, hopes and satisfactions. There are no regrets. He feels as if he gave all that he was willing to give. "I could have played for 10 more years, riding busses, hopping from town to town in hopes of catching on. I decided there were other things I could do."

Sometimes the path we take toward one dream actually leads to another. It creates a fascinating and exciting journey. Are you open to this possibility?

Where you go with your dreams depends on the price you're willing to pay. Keeping this in mind, there is a final life that may be the most exciting one of all…

The Life We Can Create. The fourth life is the one that has yet to happen. Creating the life you love is a journey of time, experience and making choices that bring satisfaction to the soul. The life yet to live is filled with every possibility – but, you must be willing to pay whatever price is necessary to have life *your way*. Here's the cool thing, and this is especially good news for those with ADHD…you *are not* bound by your past. Life is happening right *now*!

What do you want? Where do you want to go? Who do you want to hang around with, have as friends, have as a mentor, or have as customers or an audience? Answering these questions form the basis of your creative vision. The "how" part of the equation will come. Through your commitment. Doors will open.

Another cool thing is this: like my friend, who gave 98% of himself to the attainment of one dream, new opportunity came his way because of his initial path. The same will be true for your journey, as well. However, to meet those opportunities, you must focus your attention on the goal, and what lies immediately before you. You'll need to throw your entire self into achieving that next task. Eventually, as you progress, a new challenge may come to you – and you'll need to make a decision. Your choice determines the course of your life from that point forward…until another new challenge lands in your lap.

And, you have yet another opportunity to make choices that propel you onward..

Exercise #1: Four Lives

Write your biography. Looking back with scientific objectivity in an honest, rubber-meets-the-road fashion can be extremely beneficial. You'll see patterns emerge. Are these patterns helpful in venturing into the life you create? Or, have they de-railed your quest? Understanding who you have been, and why, helps you get clear on what needs to change, what you should pay attention to, and which strengths you can fall upon and use.

What are your 4 lives? Break your biography into four sections:

The Life You Could Have Had. What were your dreams growing up? Coming out of high school or college? As you progressed through life? Which dreams did you give up? What could have been? Detach yourself as you write – don't get hung up. Just describe the dream you had for your life. We'll use these dreams later.

The Life You've Learned With. What have been your major patterns, key events and decisions? In what ways did you limit yourself? What are your strong points? How well have you used these strengths? What did you decide about life?

The Life You Have Now. What works and what doesn't? Are you satisfied, unsatisfied, comfortable, bored? Where are you at now? Is this *truly* the life you love? Maybe you love 80% of your life…what about the other 20%?

The Life You Create is happening right now. Every tick of the clock brings a new opportunity to create the life you've wanted. Being aware of this – accepting responsibility for *every shred* of your past, current and future life – allows you the freedom to choose differently, play to your strengths, and enjoy more fulfillment and satisfaction with life. Write your vision down on paper. Get it out of your mind and physicalize it. Give it shape and meaning. Rehearse it. Once it's committed to memory, every day experience what it is like to live inside that vision…and make it happen!

Get to work. It's never too soon to begin paying the price of admission for a life filled with passion, commitment, purpose and joy.

Exercise #2: What's Your Story?

Yes, you do have a story to tell. What is it? Over time, discover the answers to these questions. I recommend keeping a journal specifically for your family record – which also includes *your* story. Your challenge is to simply discover these stories and explore the value they may contribute to your creative journey.

Who is the Keeper of the Family Stories? Reach out to them and ask them to pass along the tales. Look into The DNA Project or Ancestry.com. You may find some extraordinary details about your ancestral family record.

As you begin collecting these stories (and recording them in your journal), begin looking for themes. What are the common threads that connect the lives of your people to you. What value can you pull from these tales? Which tales can become archetypes for you to lean upon when necessary? Commit to telling these stories to someone in your family who hasn't heard them (your children, a niece or nephew, etc.). Speaking the stories aloud has immense power. As the teller, you become part of the story.

Write your story. Do so chronologically. Detail the points of your life that were vital to your growth and development. Capture the drama of challenging times and what you did to overcome challenges, or, what you may have learned even if you didn't completely master the obstacle. Re-visit your 4 Lives. If you haven't done so already, flesh them out with more detail, giving them flair and flavor.

What are the archetypes from *your* history? Trust me, they are there.

Passion

"When I hear a man preach I like to see him act as if he's fighting bees."
---Abraham Lincoln

"Our passions are the true phoenixes; when the old one is burnt out, a new one rises
from its ashes."
---Johann Wolfgang von Goethe

What if you don't know what you want to be when you grow-up?

You've heard the bromide many times: "Follow your passion and the money will follow."

Here's the problem with that...what if you have many passions? Or, worse, what if you just don't know what your passions are?

As someone with ADHD, you likely have insatiable curiosity. There are a multitude of subjects that interest you. It's one of the hallmarks of being a Creative Type - you have many interests. The problem comes when you can't put reigns on this curiosity and focus on just one or two things.

Often we are curious about everything and end up being passionate about *nothing*. We're all over the place. Obviously, this is a challenge.

And then there are others who have actually managed to sublimate their curious urges, stuffing personal interests in favor of raising a family, committing to a career, or meeting some other worthy responsibility. For example, many women who stayed at home to raise children, care for their husbands and households, find themselves lost once the children fly off to college and their husbands have established a career, not needing the kind of support they once required.

They are left to bounce around an empty house, cleaning up because it's become habit, feeling lifeless until her husband comes home. And, even then...

I think this issue of discovering one's passion is especially acute for women - even those with careers.

While I don't want to get too far off the subject of finding one's passion, there may be a biological issue that women face that men just don't. A few years ago I was writing a white paper for one of my clients who focused on coaching female corporate executives who were going through menopause. As a part of the research, I interviewed a well known east coast obstetrician who basically said that modern medicine and its practitioners really didn't know that much about how to treat a woman during this time of her life. He said that, on an evolutionary basis, 100-200 years ago women often died before they reached menopause. Thankfully, with modern medicine and nutrition, women's life expectancies are much, much higher than those of her great-great-great grandmother.

And, with medical breakthroughs like hormone replacement therapies and other treatments that make menopause a little easier to navigate, middle-aged women can have more relief from what can be a very difficult biological phase of their lives.

Okay - on top of the craziness of menopause, add-in empty nest syndrome and the kind of reflection that comes with reaching ages 45 to 55, and many women just don't know who they are or what they want. According to many women, this is quite common. Now, consider the fact that probably 10% of the women facing this challenge also have undiagnosed ADHD...well, it's a recipe for hopelessness.

And, what about men? For men the challenges are more covert. There are a lot of "supposed to be's" with men. A man is supposed to be: strong, a good provider, successful, a paragon of stability and character.

Here's what is true: men are just as lost as women - they just don't either know it or don't talk about it.

When I was in college a friend of mine had a friend who attended UCLA. His grandfather, father and two brothers were all doctors, and they all earned perfect grades while in school – and, of course, he was expected to follow the family tradition. For three and a half years this young man earned straight-A's. He was well on his way to doing everything necessary to enter medical school. There was a problem, though.

He didn't want to be a doctor. He wanted to be an artist, but he was deathly afraid of confronting his father and upsetting the family heritage.

During his final semester he messed-up. He got a B in one of his final classes. Distraught, unable to finally just tell his father that he did not want to be a doc, he committed suicide.

"Supposed-to-be's" can be deadly. At the very least, they have the potential to kill the spirit.

When discovering and cultivating one's passions, the "supposed-to-be's" need to be flushed down the toilet. This doesn't mean we set aside our obligations and responsibilities. On the contrary, we need to fulfill them. And, we also need to keep our own intrinsic obligation to cultivate our own passions. This is one of the secrets to true happiness and fulfillment.

How do you do that?

Seems like there are a billion sites on the internet devoted to finding one's passion. From life coaches to online tests to complete multi-layered programs - with four easy payments you, too, can find your passion!

Exercise #3: Discovery

I have an easier way - and it's pretty cool because you already know what your passions are! You've just forgotten them. You just need to excavate a little, dust them off, and begin practicing them. If you discover that you have many passions, that's fine, too. Practice each of them until you land on the one or two that resonate most. Here's the formula:

Oh, before you start this...***do not write down "supposed-to's" or "should's"!!***

When you were in school, which subjects did you enjoy most?
This is not about the classes in which you got the best grades - what did you enjoy? Maybe you currently have a career in banking...but in school you loved biology. Maybe you chose to stay home with the kids - but you really enjoyed geometry. Maybe you landed in the C-suite as a corporate executive - but poetry really touched your soul. Whatever the subjects were for you, write them down.

As a child, what were your favorite play-time activities? What did you dream of being and doing?
Childhood play can have a powerful impact. Was there something that you just did over and over? Who were your playmates? What were your roles? Write this stuff down.

Do you have hobbies? What are they? Did you have hobbies that you gave up a long time ago? What were they?
Did you paint, collect coins, collect pretty travel brochures? Do you bowl, like to listen to jazz, play an instrument? Whatever you have done for pure pleasure, write it down.

What are your strengths, gifts and talents? What kinds of activities do you enjoy?
Here's where it gets tricky. Sometimes we do stuff really well, but we hate doing it. That's not what we want here. Think about activities or actions you take that you, 1) do well, and 2) that you enjoy. For example, at work you may be a great "idea person" - you like solving problems either on your own or in a team. The strength would be "generating ideas", and it could also be, "problem solving", and it could also be, "working in a team". Maybe you have a good eye for interior design, picking materials and putting furniture together in a room. Maybe you enjoy creating a household budget - thinking of creative ways to spend your household income wisely. That's a strength.

What sort of things do you do daily (or at least frequently) that you do well, and that you enjoy?

For this exercise I recommend you write down everything you can think of - and then interview several people (fellow workers, your spouse, friends) and get their take. If you're still flummoxed, there are some good skill/strength assessments you can take online.

When you experience joy, what are you most likely doing?
Think about your happiest moments - what are you doing? Are you alone or with other people? Both? Happiness is a funny thing - you don't really know you're happy until after you experience it. When you're "in the zone" you are simply enjoying what you are doing. Typically you're so immersed, so focused, and so interested in the activity that you experience a lack of self-consciousness. This is often called a "flow" experience. Looking back, when you experience this, what are you doing? Write it down.

Which subjects interest you?
Astronomy? Physics? Alternative medicine? Maybe it's horses, motorcycles, or trains? Could it be baseball, dancing or kayaking? It doesn't matter if you have delved into the subject deeply or not, identify subjects that attract you. For example, maybe you've always been fascinated by horses. Though you may never have gotten close to one, secretly you wish you could. Here's your chance to voice this. Or, maybe you watch *Dancing With The Stars* religiously. You love the flowing dresses, sexy and elegant moves...secretly you wish you could dance like them, too. Write this stuff down. Everything. Especially the secret stuff.

Okay, you now have a list of lot of great stuff. Place your lists into a table with these headings:

School Subjects
Play Activities
Hobbies
Strengths/Talents
Joyful Times
Subjects/Interest

Place each item into an appropriate column. Once you've done that, assess the table as a whole - and notice patterns. Take a look at how items in each column relate and are connected. As you see the different patterns emerge, you may find your passion hidden there. It may jump out at you right away...it may reveal some latent desires, stuff you've buried for whatever reason (and the reasons don't matter here). Take a look at this example from Brenda S., 40-something happily married woman who has worked as a customer service professional for 5 years.

School Subjects: Geometry, Poetry, World history, Journalism
Play Activities: Drawing, Dancing, Singing, Dress-up, Travel
Hobbies: Dancing, Writing, Crochet, Reading
Strengths/Talents: Research, Writing, Problem Solving
Joyful Times: Journaling, Sing in church, Trip to Argentina
Subjects/Interest: Horses, Travel, Latin Culture, Dancing, Genealogy

Do you see the patterns? Yes, there are a couple strong ones here. To make this real, we'll highlight the main pattern in italics.

School Subjects: Geometry, Poetry, World history, *Journalism*
Play Activities: Drawing, *Dancing,* Singing, Dress-up, *Travel*
Hobbies: Dancing, *Writing,* Crochet, Reading
Strengths/Talents: *Research, Writing*, Problem Solving
Joyful Times: Journaling, Sing in church, *Trip to Argentina*
Subjects/Interest: Horses, *Travel, Latin Culture, Dancing*, Genealogy

To give her life a little pizzazz, Brenda assessed that she might really enjoy starting a blog about Argentinian culture from the perspective of an American Hispanic woman seeking to find her roots. She could have chosen to simply do a genealogical survey of her family, but that didn't quite cut it. So, she's going to write about what she finds about her family, while also putting her findings into the context of a travel-like blog. From this exercise she will take action on the following (besides starting her blog): 1) Decided to take a tango class with her husband; 2) Study Argentinian horse husbandry; 3) Planning a trip to Argentina to study specific elements of the culture, and discover first-hand her historical roots.

As you do this exercise your imagination will light up with possibilities. In Brenda's sample, there are several strength/interest areas for her to explore. There's also enough variety for someone with ADHD to satisfy curiosity. Most important, this exercise leads to identifying passions, even setting a goal.

Even better, you can keep adding to your chart. Inevitably you'll discover other buried treasures you'll want to explore - and this chart provides you with structure and context.

The Big Vision.

Creating a New Tale: How Big is Your Dream

"If you're going to think, you may as well think big."
---Donald Trump

Are you living the life you want? A central theme of the creative journey is that it is a *heroic quest*. You are the hero/heroine.

Looking back upon the tales of your ancestors, can you see the heroic quests that took place? They are there. You have people that were moved to step out of their comfort zones and make a difference for themselves, their families and the world around them. Some quests will be grand in scale, while others may seem small – but still significant.

The heroic quest begins with a dream. The dream is often fueled by some deep, burning desire to do or be *something* other than what you are doing or being now. Perhaps it is fueled by an injustice done to you, your family or to society in general. Maybe it's an inner movement to translate beauty into your own unique point-of-view. Or, perhaps it's a desire to make life less difficult for yourself and others – so you invent some new mechanism or system. The deepest and most profound heroic quest is in the seeking of spiritual truth and meaning. I believe all heroic journeys contribute to this one life-long quest. The reward is illumination and fulfillment.

Like the quintessential dream of Martin Luther King, it must be sufficiently *big*. I know…if you set a goal that's too big that your mind can't accept as being a reality, you'll just spin your wheels and make zero progress. That's *so* ADHD, isn't it?

Here's the thing - a big dream is comprised of a bunch of little dreams. With the accomplishment of each small dream, you draw closer to bringing life to the big dream. In this way, your focus will be on each small step and will *not* be overwhelmed by the prospect of accomplishing the seemingly impossible. Pulling these steps together, you'll have a plan.

The plan is a starting point. As you enter into the quest, just know that steps of the plan will change. You will be continually developing your imaginative faculties to adapt, change course and push through barriers. And, with each leap you take you will gain that much more confidence in your vision and in yourself.

The journey, then, is the training ground for living your dream. And along the way you'll be creating a new tale to add to the ancestral record. So, while you are accomplishing a goal that will provide you with a deep sense of fulfillment, purpose and peace – your story will aid others in their quests that may take place in a few years, or centuries from now. In this way your unique quest becomes *eternal*.

Exercise #4: Mapping Your Heroic Quest

Each small step becomes a point of destination in your heroic quest. Drawing upon your interests and connecting with that *something* that burns inside of you, the first step is to clearly describe the big dream. Make it real. Describe it in sensual terms – sight, touch, taste, sound, emotions. Immerse yourself in the details – imagine living it.

Next, create a map with your big dream as the destination. What are the smaller steps that lead to the big dream? There will be many, and in seemingly unrelated areas of life. Brainstorm it. Write everything down, even if it seems weird. Do not edit. Do not throw anything out. Include it all.

When you have all of your steps scattered on the map, create a step-by-step plan for each small dream. Use your imagination – and make sure that each plan has a step that takes you out of your comfort zone. Your Big Dream does not exist inside your comfort zone. Thus, you must determine to take some leaps of faith. Each step of the plan will prepare you for these leaps. It helps to keep in mind that this journey was especially designed just for you. *This* heroic quest is for you to take – and for no one else.

This mapping and planning step is essential to the quest. It is a proven fact that 95% of all great accomplishments began with a written plan. Commit to starting this process *today*.

Part One Summary

You are a Creative Type, made perfectly by a perfect Creator. You were *designed* to be creative, so quit saying you aren't creative! Knock it off! You have tremendous gifts to give the world – so get to work!

By my reckoning there are 5 creative types. You fit into one or all of them depending on the circumstances. It's good to know where you fit… but also know that you aren't relegated to one class of creativity. That's the thing about being a Creative, isn't it? One moment you're riding a subway home from your job as an attorney, writing a story on yellow legal pads. The next, you've got a runaway bestseller with Hollywood knocking on your door. That's Scott Turow's story (*Presumed Innocent*). That can be you, too.

Your family stories provide you with creative DNA. Yes, you are a free person with no chains to the past, born into a caste from which there is no escape. But, your family stories provide you with a rich background that you can draw upon. If your ancestors had wild and crazy creative moments, you can, too. Learn your stories and draw confidence.

You really do have four lives. What are they? Where have you excelled? In which situations have you short-changed yourself? Can you see the patterns? How have you been hiding your creative genius? This exercise isn't meant to make you feel like a loser. On the contrary, since folk with ADHD have propensity toward low self-esteem, it's good to know where this comes from so we can stop doing those things. There are also areas in which we have absolutely shined – so we want to focus on those things and do more of the same. Our results will be better and our star will shine a little brighter. Don't be afraid of these areas in which you failed – learn from them and laugh about them…and then delight in those things you do well.

Then, think big about your life. Create a vision that's been made from the stuff of your unique genius. Think you can't do it? Think again. Albert Einstein (widely thought to have had ADHD) was a drop-out in school. He was a lowly clerk. But he had a particular genius and ripped apart the world of theoretical physics through his brilliance. Stephen King wrote his novel *Carrie* in the bathroom of the very small home he shared with his wife, Tabitha, plucking away on a toy typewriter. He threw the novel away. Tabitha rescued it and sent it to publishers. The rest is publishing history. Yes, if these "ordinary" people can do what they did, so can you. *"Whatever the mind of man can conceive, he can achieve"*. Napoleon Hill said that in his classic *Think and Grow Rich*. If you can dream it…it can be done…by you!

Once you've identified your unique genius and begun to believe that you were created perfectly by a perfect Creator, the next thing you need is specific knowledge.

Rome wasn't built in a day, and neither will your dreams come true by wishing them into existence. You need knowledge about your specific genius, and how to get things done.

Part Two: Knowledge is Power

On the Road to Canaan

It is a rough road that leads to the heights of greatness.
---Seneca

"Whoever undertakes to set himself up as a judge of Truth and Knowledge is shipwrecked by the laughter of the gods."
---Albert Einstein

"To know, is to know that you know nothing. That is the meaning of true knowledge."
---Socrates

If you come to a fork in the road, take it.
——-Yogi Berra

Creative Power Begins with Knowledge

Thomas Keller - Mastering the Basics

> *"A first-rate soup is more creative than a second-rate painting."*
> ---**Abraham Maslow**

I love good food. While I'd never turn down an In 'n' Out cheeseburger, there's something to be said for having a food "experience".

Such is the case with The French Laundry in Yountville, CA. Named the best restaurant in the United States in 2003 by *Restaurant Magazine* and one of just a handful of restaurants in the U.S. to receive three stars from the Michelin Guide, The French Laundry has earned its world-wide renown due to owner and Master Chef Thomas Keller's quest for perfection.

With a plethora of chefs receiving celebrity status due to the popularity of The Food Network (i.e. Emeril Lagasse, Rachel Ray) and the surge of reality-based 16-week personality-infused cook-off television shows like Iron Chef, the interest in cooking has never been higher than it is right now. Being a chef has become cool. And, in the world of master chefs, Thomas Keller is *the* star.

He's the only chef in the U.S. to have two three-star Michelin rated restaurants in America (the other is *Per Se* in New York). His Bouchon restaurants (Yountville, New York, Beverly Hills and Las Vegas), and Ad-Hoc in Yountville, all receive the highest praise from customers and critics alike. He also operates the Bouchon Bakery in each of the aforementioned cities (from which the Almond Strawberry Croissant will cause you to see the face of Jesus. Yes, I swear by Heaven and Earth, it's that good).

I became fascinated with Keller after reading *The Soul of a Chef* by Michael Ruhlman. While *Soul of a Chef* inspired me to become a better cook, and is perhaps one of the best books I've ever read about practical creativity, it was the section on Keller that grabbed my attention.

With great chefs we often get caught up in the extravagant meals they prepare. Without a doubt The French Laundry may well have some of the most inventive chefs in the business. But, Keller is a fan of Bistro food, common food, made with just a few accessible ingredients, prepared to absolute perfection. For example, his favorite meal (though he says it's impossible to choose just one) is roasted chicken with a dinner salad. His favorite burger: In 'n' Out. Simplicity, it seems, is the essential ingredient to greatness. And, what makes Keller so great is his absolute commitment to the fundamentals.

Like a great athlete, artist or entrepreneur, the best in their professions practice the fundamentals rigorously. Whatever the particular set of fundamentals may be, they form the backbone of their work. According to Keller, the key to becoming a great cook is repetition. Doing an action over and over again, day in, day out, establishes the foundation for greatness.

"I think what is really paramount to becoming a top chef is desire. People talk about passion as being something that's overriding. Passion comes and goes. It ebbs and flows. We can be passionate one day about something and not the next day. A top chef must have that strong everlasting burning desire inside to continue to pursue long-term goals. Another essential quality that a top chef must have is the ambition to achieve greatness."

Keller's quote provides the gateway to taking the creative route. Where is your desire focused? What drives your commitment? Do you have a burning desire to achieve something worthwhile? Do you have the ambition to do something with greatness?

As you ponder these questions, you might want to think about greatness in terms of throwing a dinner party. You make your best recipe, one that is so embedded in your memory that grilling the shallots and heating the Mornay sauce to the perfect temperature are like breathing—it just happens automatically. As you broil tenderloin wrapped in a flaky brioche to melt-in-your-mouth tenderness, you reflect on why you give your best, and why you have spent countless hours practicing time-honored culinary techniques. You derive great joy and satisfaction from cooking. *But, there's something else.*

It's the joyful faces of your guests as they share the meal. Greatness can only come by cooking for others. But - and this is important - you're not doing it to gain approval or even to achieve greatness, but to truly serve others. That's the most important fundamental of all.

While you consider your calling, also think about the fundamentals that are attached to this Calling. **Commit** to them whole-heartedly. **Practice** until they are trained not just to memory, but become a part of you. **Integrate** the overriding value that makes one great - *you are doing this for the benefit of others while also satisfying a deep drive within you.* Do it well, and you will be *assigned* greatness by those whom you serve. It's a lesson that Thomas Keller, the greatest chef in the world, has never forgotten.

Exercise #5: Preparing Your Saddle-Bags: The Individual Learning Plan

My friend Michelle Payne, Executive Coach supreme, is an advocate for an organization that specializes in helping parents take a priority role in their kid's education. Innovative Education Management made its mark as a champion for the charter school movement in California. Its founder, Randy Gaschler, took a no-prisoners approach to locking horns with the California Department of Education and the other powers that had effectively cut parents out of the loop.

One of the things that IEM endorses is the use of Individual Learning Plans. ILP's have been around for a while, and they are commonly used as a professional development tool by firms in the United Kingdom. Within the charter and home school system, ILP's are used to design a child's education - identifying subjects, courses of action, and the means to track progress in helping a kid learn.

The point of an ILP is to increase knowledge. And, when it comes to unleashing your full creative potential, knowledge is the mortar that holds everything together.

Anyone interested in tapping their true creative power might want to consider creating an ILP. It's pretty simple, and it looks a lot like goal-setting. But, it's focused entirely on acquiring knowledge.

People with ADHD can derive substantial benefit from an ILP. If you're like me, you're curious about a lot of things. When doing research for something it's very easy for me to get lost in that research while working on a project. What can happen is that I "rabbit trail" so much that I don't get anything done and fall behind. The ILP can help keep this from happening because you determine a knowledge plan and stick to it. Of course, sticking to it is the thing…

Here are the simple steps you can take to create an ILP:

Identify your learning goal. Rochelle is a healing touch practitioner. While she likes working on people, she's become fascinated with healing animals. Her goal is to learn how she can apply her craft to the healing of animals (in particular, horses).

Set a time schedule. Set a time-frame for acquiring your knowledge. Realistically, any subject you might choose could take a lifetime of constant learning. In fact, being a life-long learner is a trait *all* creative-types share. So, your time-frame can be somewhat loose (like Rochelle, she hasn't set a specific time goal. She understands what makes her tick, and for her the learning is a part of the journey). Or, you can be very specific, especially if your knowledge acquisition is tied to another time-sensitive goal. For example, let's say you want to write an article for a trade journal. The deadline is in two months. To write it, you need to acquire some additional knowledge. The external deadline essentially sets your time-frame.

Create action steps for each goal. Rochelle began by reading a book. Then, by chance, she was attending a horse event and came across a local ranch that specialized in healing draft horses that had been abused. They offered a class (which Rochelle completed). She also found a local woman who specializes in healing animals through energy work. Rochelle initiated contact with her. Thus, her steps here have been: a) Read about the subject, b) Take a class, and c) Find an expert mentor. In her case, because she has placed intention in her quest for knowledge, and she's attuned to opportunity, her steps are revealed as she goes. In essence, her curiosity is her action plan - and her willingness to initiate action. Her process is very intuitive - it's a part of her organic creativity. I'm a little different. For some things I need a step-by-step plan to acquire knowledge, while other pursuits I can simply go where the path leads.

Identify your resources. As in Rochelle's situation, she came upon one of her resources by chance. But, she also put herself in an environment where resources were potentially available. She' also gone online and researched the heck out of the subject (that's how she found the local expert - who, coincidentally, wrote the book she had read about healing critters!). There is a wealth of resources at your fingertips on the internet, at a bookstore or library, even in the Yellow Pages. Friends, associates and family can also help. So, make a list. Keep track of them all.

Keep a learning journal. You might want to keep separate journals for different subjects. As you dive into your subject you'll want to keep track of all the nuggets of information you acquire and where you found it (i.e. keeping track of your resources). Over time you'll integrate all this information into knowledge - especially as you apply it to whatever you're doing.

That's what an Individual Learning Plan looks like. There are many formats - and some can be quite complex. But, I like keeping things simple. While acquiring knowledge isn't necessarily easy, the plan you use doesn't have to be difficult. The key is to have insight about how you learn and what will make the process enjoyable.

Exercise #6: What's the plan, Stan?

"He who fails to plan is planning to fail."
  —-Winston Churchill

There is a common misconception that a Creative Type can just stand at her easel or sit in the workshop and *turn it on*. Like Mozart (another thought to have ADHD), the musician will sit at the piano and symphonies will suddenly flow perfectly into his mind and, magically, four or five hours a completed work of genius will be ready to be shipped off to the New York Philharmonic.

It doesn't happen that way for mere mortals. They call it a creative *process* for a reason. And, like any process, planning is important to the outcome.

It's common sense that success is planned. This doesn't mean there's no room for spontaneity. There is. But, the process as a whole is planned. And, believe it or not, this is a good thing for us Creative Types.

Most of the Creatives I know are *not* ultra organized. And that's okay, so long as one has a system and can synthesize a vision into a goal. According to many, the best goal planning approach happens to be SMART. When you get serious about bringing your vision to life, keep the SMART goal setting formula in mind.

Specific: Your goal needs to be specific. Being vague doesn't work. For example, a vague goal is "I am going to be a writer". A specific goal is, "I'm going to write a novel about the lives of British missionaries in China during the Communist revolution."

Measurable: There needs to be a way of measuring what you do. If I'm writing a book, I'll shoot for the number of words that will be in this book. For a novel, maybe 60,000 words is a good number. When I get to that word count I should be done.

Attainable: Does writing a novel seem overwhelming? Maybe. But, can you write 3 pages per day? 5 pages per day? One single page per day? Of course you can! That's how a novel is written – one page at a time. To get there, I might set a daily objective of writing 500 words per day. In this profile it will take 120 days of writing to meet the goal.

Realistic: Is it realistic for you to write a novel? Maybe, maybe not.

Here's the thing, Picasso said the chief enemy of creativity is "common sense". It is NOT realistic to be a Creative Type! You will face all kinds of overt and covert resistance. But, you ARE a Creative Type…therefore it is unrealistic for you to *not* create. Let go of conventions and safety. Write! Paint! Dance! Do what you love to do! Have *un*common sense.

Timely: Here's where the rubber meets the road. If your novel is 60,000 words, then you will have about 340 pages of double-spaced copy. If you complete an average of 5 pages per day, it will take you 68 days to finish your first draft. Three pages per day will take you 113 days. How many days per week will you write? If you write three days per week, three pages per day (3/3), it will take you nine months to finish. Three days per week at five pages per day (3/5), five months. The pace is up to you. The advice? Here is where reality hits – start conservative and then build momentum. You may start at 3/3, move to 3/5 and end up at 5/5 – and finish in four months. Whatever you do, choose an end date based upon your initial projection – and stick to your schedule! This is essential for people with ADHD! No matter what – keep your schedule!

Becoming Self-Less

The Wisdom of 16 Year Olds

I love our daughter, Shannon. She's 22, smart, funny and wise beyond her years. I learn a lot from her. She just graduated from college, and she's retained a healthy dose of what she was like when she was 16 – a spirit of adventure.

One of the things I like best about Shannon is that she and her friends will just go ahead and do something if they think it's cool. They don't stop to think about whether it'll sell or not, if people will like it, how hard it might be, etc.

If it's cool, they just do it.

As adults we sometimes forget about this wisdom. We get burdened with all the practical realities.

Much to their credit, 16-year olds don't. If it looks like fun, they give it a try. Especially with the creative stuff. Now, we're blessed that Shannon really gets right from wrong, what's in her best interests and so forth. So, we don't have to worry about the reckless kind of "let's go for it" attitude. She's not going to do things that will hurt her or her friends.

Instead, she surrounded herself with other creative, art-music-writing loving kids who see the world in unique, often amazing ways. They appreciate things like sunsets, old movies and actually like the music we listened to when we were their age. They're literate. In fact, one year my wife and I were helping Shannon study for an art appreciation class, showing her a series of 100 flashcards of different works of art. We were blown away. Not only did she know the name of the piece, but the artist and the year it was created.

More and more I'm seeing these kids being shaped in a well-rounded education, in which art, science, literature, history and math all have value. It's a good thing. We're going to need this kind of breadth from the citizenry and our leaders in the decades to come.

So, when I think of them, I know the world will be in good hands...so long as they hold onto the wisdom they have now.

Exiting the comfort zone.

Imagine that you're sitting comfortably in a great big La-Z-Boy recliner, a cool beverage in-hand, watching *Casablanca* for the 100th time on TCM. You're feeling good. The safety and reliability of home wraps around you like a quilt your grandmother hand-stitched 50 years ago. This is your zone. The comfort zone. And you could stay here forever.

Now, imagine you're in a small office. The only furnishings are a government-issue metal desk, a metal folding chair and a phone sitting atop the desk. Next to the phone is a stack of white 81/2 x 11 sheets of paper. Each sheet has a list of names with a phone number next to each name. Your job? You must make a *cold call* to every name on those sheets of paper.

Yes, you have now exited the comfort zone (no one likes to cold call, right?).

Every one of us has exited the comfort zone. First day of kindergarten; first date; a job interview. If you're breathing, you've done it.

A curious thing happens at about age 35. We start settling into our life (remember Our 4 Lives? This is the one you live with). Marriage, mortgage, kids, a steady job that we can't afford to lose. We take the kids to Disneyland for our vacation; take the boat to the lake on weekends in the summer, watch football in the fall, and we still enjoy holding our spouse's hand 20 years into the marriage. It's intoxicatingly pleasant. Of course, this may seem like a far-fetched fantasy for someone with ADHD. It's so chaos-free and, to some, kind of boring. There's nothing at all wrong with this life. However…

Even for "normal" people it can be creatively numbing, acting like a sedative for the creative soul. It's so easy to slip into the comfort zone and not realize that 15 or 20 or 50 years have passed. And so have a billion opportunities to take risks that could have provided significant added -value to life while you're grilling wieners in the back yard. *The Life We Could Have Had* begins to gnaw, resulting in high blood pressure, belly fat and a second on the house.

Here's the good news: the *Life You Could Have* is *always* available to you – no matter how old or young you are.

But, that life requires you to *do* something – you must step out of the comfort zone.

You'll have to endure the butterflies in the stomach, sweaty palms, nervous tension that accompanies the exit from living the La-Z-Boy life.

That's a good thing. The nerves tell you that you're moving in the right direction. Human nature is such that fear typically is the companion of risk and entering the unknown. Progress is determined by how well we move through the fear.

Think about your dreams for a moment and compare that vision to your current reality. Which life do you think will bring more satisfaction and happiness? Or, at the very least, how much more value will taking a step outside the lines bring to the current life you live?

Be honest...is that life worth feeling a few butterflies?

You can minimize the discomfort. Planning, Practice and Patience – the 3 -P Approach – can help tame even the most knee-rattling jitters. Apply the 3-P Approach to the goal that's currently in front of you.

Planning. Achieving a goal requires many steps. Break them out into small, highly focused progressions. Write them down. As you do, you'll be able to pin-point those steps that will require an exit from the comfort zone. Each of those progression points is a growth moment, where true progress will be made.

Practice. As you get close to one of those progression points, practice or rehearse what you'll be doing. Simulate the actions. If it's a cold call, practice your script. Ask a friend to help – rehearse your script over the phone. Ditto with a job interview or any other action that requires talking to a stranger (or a bunch of strangers – like giving a speech). If it's a physical activity, be faithful with your training. Do visioning practice – imagine yourself performing the action perfectly. If it's an art, keep painting-writing-dancing-acting until techniques become like breathing.

Patience. If things don't go perfectly, be patient. Don't beat yourself up. Take the experience and learn from it. Don't worry if things don't go perfectly as planned – just keep moving forward.

Something else here – what makes this a lot easier, too, is a supportive spouse, significant other or a supportive friend. They can be there for you when your confidence flags, or you're feeling scared. I have been blessed with a spouse who "gets" my need to create. She supports me. I don't have to make excuses to take long drives so I can park myself at an internet café and pump out my five pages per day. As you prepare, include your significant other in the process. It really helps – and, believe me, they may want more for you than you realize. They'll be your biggest advocate and cheerleader.

And that's especially helpful when you're in the process of acquiring knowledge. Another asset in your quest is to find your Yoda...a person who is an expert in their field who would be willing to teach and guide you. You begin that by considering apprenticeship...

Apprenticeship.

Earning your stripes

"The mistakes one makes are the dues to be paid in order to have a full life."
—Sophia Loren

No one ever said it would be easy. In fact, the notion of an "overnight sensation" is vastly over-stated. There are very few people gifted enough to go from obscurity to stardom in a short time. (Note: Yes, instant stardom *can* be achieved via U-Tube, but, it's very, very, very rare).

Thomas Edison failed 10,000 times before inventing the light bulb.

It took Jonas Salk and a crack team of researchers seven years to create a vaccine against polio.

Famously, Mozart's genius wasn't recognized in his own time by most; numerous Delta blues musicians played ramshackle juke joints in the south during the 1920's and 30's, long before the British Wave guitar slingers of the 1960's discovered the genius of legends like Robert Johnson and Son House.

Bill Walsh, the legendary coach of the San Francisco 49ers, who was nicknamed "The Genius", was an assistant coach in college and at the pro level for many years before taking over the worst team in the NFL - and then going on to win three Super Bowls.

The stories of Creative Types pounding the pavement, playing smoky backwater bars, toiling at their inventions late into the night in their garage, are many. And they all speak to one thing.

You've got to earn your stripes. Paying your dues is necessary if you are going to succeed at anything. For a lot of ADHDers this is difficult. First, paying one's dues requires discipline – which can be a challenge. Throughout this book are numerous techniques for developing discipline without sacrificing curiosity. Second, for most people with ADHD, they have been stifled by varying institutions –failing in school, floating from job to job, experiencing multiple failed relationships. It's as if we come pre-loaded with low self-esteem, destined to fail.

But, fear not. Trust in your creative gifts. They are, among many things, the qualities that make you special, unique and exceptional. Remember, you are perfect as you are.

Earning your stripes is about practicing your art or skills until your mind is numb and your fingers bleed. I know an 18 year old kid who is one of the most gifted guitar players I've ever heard. He wants to be a session musician - so he practices six hours every day.

It is common knowledge in baseball that a pitcher needs to throw 500 innings and a hitter needs 1,000 at-bats in the minor leagues before they're ready to go to *The Show*.

But, as we earn our stripes, we don't have to go it alone.

During the Middle Ages a movement in commerce took shape in which guilds were formed. A distant ancestor to today's labor unions, guilds were a necessary step one had to take in order to become a certain type of craftsman.

Artists, builders, scientists and many other professions have apprentices who do much of the grunt work. It's like being a young designer who works for Ralph Lauren. The head honcho may sketch out designs for a whole line, presenting the ideas he wants to communicate, the aesthetics that must be presented. Junior designers take it over and create the mechanicals that are then passed down to the folk who make the garments. These designers earn their stripes by being apprentices to Lauren (or Lauren's head designers).

Today the idea of mentoring has caught fire. From school children to business executives, formalized mentorship programs are popping up everywhere. There's good reason. Mentorship, when done properly, works.

Typically the mentor is someone who is older, wiser and seasoned in the field. They have accumulated knowledge, accomplishments and reputation. Their role is to meet with their mentee on a regular basis, offer suggestions and direction, utilize their network of contacts for the benefit of the mentee, and generally, "raise their mentee up".

As the mentee, your role is to listen, learn, practice obedience and be coachable. The mentor is giving something of him or herself, and you are expected to do the same. In fact, quite often this isn't a one-way process...the mentor can learn as much from the mentee.

Having a mentor is valuable in any endeavor. Over the course of a career, it is possible to have a number of mentors. The fact of the matter is that no one is "self-made". We all have teachers, people who support us, believe in us, and want us to succeed. And, all too frequently, our mentors are not members of our family or are close friends. Friendship may develop over time, but generally there is a degree of separation. It is human nature to trust the third-party or "outside" expert versus those close to us.

There are potential mentors in every field. In college or grad school, a professor can be a mentor. In business, an older more experienced executive or tradesman. In art, it could be an acting coach, master artist, master gardener, master chef - you get the idea.

The best way to find the right mentor for you is to do your homework. If you've settled upon your chosen field, undertake this process:

Survey all of the literature written about your field. Check out books, journals, websites, blogs, magazines, videos. Which names keep rising to the top? Where are they located? Also check out companies, associations and clubs close to you. There's bound to be someone local who has a good reputation, is well respected, published, and is held in high esteem.

Contact local associations, clubs, etc. and ask if there are 3 or 4 people locally who are considered experts in their field. Ask the official about the character traits of each person. Chances are they'll be able to give you some solid background.

Investigate further. Go online and Google each of the names. You should be able to find everything from a resume to published writings, even commentary from their peers.

Narrow it down to 2 or 3 and - *gulp* **- call them to make an appointment**. The higher up they are in a company, the harder it will be to reach them. Keep at it. And make sure the person screening their calls knows you aren't selling anything. Also, seek permission to e-mail them. You might even want to send a personal letter. While e-mails from unknowns are often zapped, every piece of mail is typically opened and read.

When you get the appointment, be prepared (the 3-P Approach). Have some pointed questions ready. You are not prepared to ask this person to mentor you at this time - you may not even like him or her (and chemistry can be important). Ask questions about the field, the specialized knowledge required. Ask about their careers and how they became who they are. The final line of questions to ask are these: "Did you have a mentor? Who were they? What was the most valuable thing you learned from them?" Finally, "Are you willing to be a mentor, or can you recommend someone who could be a good mentor?"

Once you've narrowed it down to your favorite, make the call. **Ask**. They'll say "yes" or "no" or refer you to someone else. If they say "no", thank them for their time, and move on to your next favorite.

Eventually you'll find the mentor that's right for you. Sometimes you may have to pay for mentorship (e.g. through an executive coach or coach-consultant), or take a class from them. But, they might be tickled to be your mentor. Despite their level of accomplishment, you might be surprised at how few requests they may receive "out of the blue". They may mentor someone inside their organization, but there's something special about you taking the time to seek them out.

After all, no matter how accomplished, your mentor is also human. He or she likes to feel special and important. Because you sought them out, your respect for them will be clearly communicated and evident.

When a potential mentor shows interest, it will be important for you to be forthcoming about your ADHD. You need to share the areas in which you are challenged, your successes and failures in managing your condition, the systems you have in place, your support system that is in place, etc. Be candid and answer every question asked. Your mentor is taking you on because they care about you – so, don't let ADHD be a surprise to them.

Thank You, Jimi Hendrix

"Blues is easy to play, but hard to feel"
---**Jimi Hendrix**

"I've been imitated so well I've heard people copy my mistakes."
——**Jimi Hendrix**

I may be an old guy, but I like to rock. I was reared on Aerosmith, Hendrix and Led Zeppelin. While my appreciation for other music, Classical to country, has grown over time, bluesy rock and roll is what still ignites my creative spirit.

The musician whom I most admire has always been Jimi Hendrix. Rightfully, most know him as the pioneering creative genius that combined fuzz, distortion and feedback into a new musical form. He changed the musical landscape of the latter half of the 20th century. From Keith Richards and Eric Clapton to Social Distortion and Fall Out Boy, he continues to influence musicians in every genre. In fact, *Rolling Stone Magazine* listed him as the greatest guitar player in rock history.

At his heart, though, Hendrix was a bluesman. He cut his teeth playing in the bands for Ike & Tina Turner, the Isley Brothers and Little Richard, and was heavily influenced by Muddy Waters, Howlin' Wolf and Robert Johnson. Long before Hendrix was *Hendrix* he had mastered the 12-bar chord progression that is fundamental to the blues and jazz.

Hendrix couldn't read or write music. Like so many of the blues greats, he learned by ear, and mastered by practice. He was well known for his all night jam sessions in which he would take a simple combination of blues riffs and ignite them into a 20-minute explosion of searing, boundary-breaking sound. His greatness came from his absolute commitment to his guitar and the blistering sounds that came from his Marshall stack.

Musically the only thing I can play is a stereo. But, Hendrix has had a significant influence on my approach to writing. From him I've learned rhythm and riff, and apply this in varying degrees to whatever work I'm doing. And the more I learned about Hendrix, the more curious I became about the history of the blues and all of the great blues players that came before him. The cascading effect has been profound because the blues isn't just music, it's something you feel. It speaks to and from the soul.

Given this, your mentors can actually be anyone who has left their mark on culture. There will be a historical record of their life – and you have access to their record and the wisdom of their life. Forming a kind of "super mentor team" comprised of accomplished people can be very helpful in your quest. Study them. Learn about not only what they accomplished, but how they failed – and then handled the failure. Pay attention to what their lives can contribute to your journey.

Exercise #7: Your Personal Board of Directors

The masters I admire come from many fields. Ernest Hemmingway, Jack Kerouac, Jimi Hendrix and Thomas Keller are a few of the people whom I not only admire, but have studied. Their lives and their approach to their craft has taught me more than what I ever could have learned sitting in a classroom.

Have you really thought about who your masters are? What is it about them that inspires, teaches, transforms? Fundamentally, what makes them different than others in their field? What can you learn from them that you could learn from no one else?

Take a little time and think about these questions and then supply some answers you can draw upon that will deepen your experience, add to your knowledge and, in the long run, help you cultivate more meaning and fulfillment from what you do.

The master(s) you admire most:

What do you admire about them?

When it comes to fundamentals, what skills, abilities or techniques have they mastered that you must still work on?

How did they go about applying the fundamentals differently than others?

Your commitment: what, how and when will you begin practicing these things?

Environment

Your Special Place

"Time is the coin of your life. It is the only coin you have, and only you can determine how it will be spent. Be careful lest you let other people spend it for you."
—-**Carl Sandburg**

An iron French key. Two polished stones and a three-inch fluorite obelisk. Steve Carlton and Don Sutton baseball cards and a natural wood golf tee. A small, flat, clear stone with the word "Create" etched into it. A purple conch shell. Two postcards: a "Fly to the South Sea Isles Pan American World Airways", and one of an Alien wearing a cowboy hat, Wrangler clad legs crossed and boots resting on the dashboard of his convertible. A bookmark with a photo of my recently departed grandmother. Photos of my wife, daughter and dog. Art work my daughter made when she was in 2nd grade. A piece of tan sandstone with million-year-old fish fossil stamped into it. A polished fossilzed granite tray. Hanging from the corner of a bookcase are a Celtic cross on a heavy gold chain, two small silver crosses and silver brooch with inlaid Afghani turquoise attached to a black leather strap.

These are my touchstones and mementos. All have meaning to me. All inspire me in some way. They are all at my writing desk, the place where I create.

When I need a kick in the butt to get going, I look to the cards of Sutton and Carlton. Steve Carlton was one of the most intelligent ball-players of his era, while Don Sutton created success through hard work, grit and a nasty over-hand 12/6 curveball. These were my idols when I played ball.

I look to the alien cowboy when I need a boost of originality. The fossils and stones ground me when I'm getting too out-there.

The French key reminds me that every locked door can be opened. The crosses remind me to ask, seek and knock - and also help me keep perspective. I may not have all the answers, but God *does*.

These small items are fun tools that make sitting at my desk 5-8 hours a day a little more interesting. But, magic only comes by having faith in a vision much larger than myself, and in working hard toward the accomplishment of that vision.

Objects have as much power as we give to them. They are physical manifestations of ideas and values that we may hold dear. I encourage their use, especially by Creative Types. Anything we can use to get rolling is beneficial. You see, you will fight many battles. They will come from external sources (like family, the need to pay bills, health concerns, etc), but the really tough ones will come from within. There will be resistance. There will be doubts. There will be distractions. So you need every advantage you can get. This is especially true for those of us with ADHD.

Sometimes when we reach a point of blockage, our brains can just shut down. Taking a deep breath and a few moments to study what's around us, familiar items that bring back good memories, moments of triumph, or just make us feel happy can give the mind enough time to re-load. And then we're off again, focused on our quest.

Mementos and special objects can help create the right environment to be productive - and environment is important.

The "where" of creativity can be any place. In your home or work office, at the kitchen table, in a park or sidewalk cafe, or even riding a subway. What matters is that you have some degree of comfort, safety and security.

I do my best writing in my home office. I am surrounded by familiar things, people who care about me, reference material, art on the walls, mementos. Maybe something like this will work for you, too. Maybe you need to create a space. Perhaps for you it's important to just get away to catch the Muse and put her to work. There are artist and writer's colonies where Creative Types go to find a peaceful place to work, surrounded by other Creatives. It can be an energy thing, too. Maybe that's why so many artists assemble in places like Santa Fe, Taos or Sedona. Maybe we just convince ourselves that places like those are necessary.

It's a personal thing. To me, it's about being where you are – create where you are. And, wherever you may be, carve out an environment that works. If you're in Cleveland you don't have to move to New Mexico to find the Muse. She's there with you on the Erie shores.

As fashionista Tim Gunn says, "Make it work."

Because, wherever you are, that's where you'll find your creative thunder.

Exercise #8: Where Do You Create?

Time, community, internal focus – all contribute to your environment. For creative-types, environment is incredibly important. It becomes the workshop of your soul.

If you had the perfect environment, what would it look like? Where is it? Aesthetically, does it truly reflect who you are? How much time do you spend there?

What is your environment like now? What's the difference between where you're at now and your perfect environment?

What's keeping you from moving from here to there?

Make a plan to create the perfect environment. Prioritize the steps.

Take the first step.

Today.

Right *now*.

People

The Support of a Good Woman (or Man)

"A psychiatrist asks a lot of expensive questions your wife asks for nothing."
---**Joey Adams**

Yes, it's true. Behind every successful man (or woman), there is a good woman (or man).

When I was a much younger man working at an advertising agency in Texas, one day the president of our company was discussing who his best account executives were. "Without question, our best AE's are women whose husbands stand behind them one-hundred percent. Selling is a tough business, and without that support they wouldn't succeed."

Of course, he was right. Selling is as creative a business as there is. A good account executive must be innovative, be able to think on her feet, design proposals that capture and enroll, and of course, be able to withstand massive amounts of rejection.

It has a lot in common with any type of creative endeavor.

I am blessed to have a wife who not only supports me, but actively encourages me and challenges me to be my best. When I feel defeated, she tells me how good I am. She builds up my confidence – something very important most with ADHD need.

But, she is also honest with me. She edits most everything I write, and so – because she wants me to be my best – she doesn't pull punches when reviewing my work. I *need* her honesty. Sometimes we disagree over content. Most of the time she's right on target. Sometimes I keep what I've written because, well, we just see the world differently at times.

But, her point-of-view is valid and necessary. She challenges me to see things from multiple perspectives, not just my own. And that's important for every Creative Type. However, while she will occasionally challenge me, she also respects my vision of the world. My brain is wired differently – and she knows that.

Because of her I don't create in a vacuum. I can get pretty "out there" sometimes, and she brings me back to earth.

When my work moves her, she tells me. And that keeps me going. You see, while I do write for myself first and foremost, I also write for her. She is my audience – my best ally, editor and friend.

Do you get this kind of support from your spouse or significant other? If not, can this be cultivated? Can you pour your heart out about your need to create, and will they listen and open their heart to you?

If they truly love you, they will. Maybe they won't understand completely, but that's okay. What you want is for them to be your cheerleader.

But, if you don't have that, there are other ways to attain the support you need. I once went through a period of my life in which I did not have Debbie in my life. I was alone. I found my support among friends who were also writers.

Hanging at Morning Thunder Café

"In everyone's life, at some time, our inner fire goes out. It is then burst into flame by an encounter with another human being. We should all be thankful for those people who rekindle the inner spirit."
---Albert Schweitzer

In 1989 I took a job running a tourism bureau in a secluded county in northeastern California. It didn't pay much, but it provided the opportunity to return to the place where I grew up. It also gave me the opportunity to put my skills to use in giving something back to the community that had given so much to me.

I rented the second storey of an old Victorian home. The exterior walls of the living and bedrooms were dominated by large windows that looked out upon a canopy of oak, maple, cedar and pine. Best of all, it was quietly serene.

The 18 months I spent there was one of the most creatively productive times of my life. Writing poetry on yellow legal pads. Banging out a novel on an old IBM Selectric typewriter. I was happily unattached and enjoying my life.

One of those pleasures was meeting once per month with a group of writer friends at the Morning Thunder Café. We'd come together and share what we had written over the past month. We also shared and laughed about the rejections we may have received from heartless, unimaginative editors. We talked about our lives.

Having that group of friends was important to my development as a writer. A supportive group of people to share the travails, joys and inspirations of the writing life was a way of connecting with others who shared a passion. It was community.

It meant I was never alone. I didn't create in a vacuum.

When you enter into the creative life, not everyone – especially those who love you – will necessarily be supportive. Either they don't really understand, don't want you to get hurt, or they fear that you will change (and the creative life will change you). One of two things usually happens: either you will cut-off your dream of being a fashion designer at the knees, or you'll become a Closet Creative, typing your novel while hiding in the closet under the stairs where no one can find you.

Creating in secret isn't that much fun. That is why having a circle of people around you who understand is critical. The act of creation is up to *you* and you alone. Connection with other Creative Types makes the journey a little easier and far more enjoyable.

That's the emotional benefit. The other benefit is that you learn from the others.

As my friends would recite their works and we'd discuss the piece, I'd pick up little things – techniques, phrasing, perspective. I learned to see the world through other artistic eyes, go beyond my limited vision. These evenings at Morning Thunder were some of the most valuable in my creative life.

Do you have a community? Who provides support? Which people encourage you to do what you love and were meant to do? Who pushes you to get better?

Find your Morning Thunder crew. They'll be some of the best friends you've ever had.

Time

Does Anybody Really Know What Time It Is? Does Anybody Really Care?

"They say time changes things, but you actually have to change them yourself"
—**Andy Warhol**

"If you're not early, you're late."
—**Ed Foreman**

"The only reason for time to exist is so that everything doesn't happen at once."
—**Albert Einstein**

Does anyone care what time it is? Yes. You do.

However, time can be measured in a number of ways. The trick is finding the time orientation that works for you. For people with ADHD this is important. You see, an ADHD coach told once me that people with our unique condition took twice as long to get something done than "normal" people. I didn't believe him at first. To prove him wrong I began tracking my time by the minute for each project I was working on. Guess what? For a small project that "should" have taken an hour, took 90 minutes. Something that I estimated 4-5 hours actually took 8-10. I proved him right.

Your approach to time is essential. How will you track it?

For example, a news editor measures time by the minute, especially when it comes to reporters meeting deadlines. Contractors measure time according to completion dates in their contract. If they are late, it costs them money. A new parent gauges time by the sound of their hungry baby crying. A writer may measure time by the number of pages he writes each day. There are a lot of ways to measure and track time.

I read a story about the Hopi Indians and their relationship to time. Almost a century ago the government wanted to implement a series of building projects on reservation land in New Mexico. In return for letting the Federals do their building projects, the Hopi were promised jobs - and they agreed to allow the projects to move forward.

Of course, the projects did move forward and no Hopi's were hired. Rather than complaining, protesting or rescinding permission to let the projects continue, the Elders simply said, "One day they will need us again and we will remember this betrayal."

Two *generations* later the Federals were knocking on the door again. This time they wanted to build a dam. Even though none of the Hopi's charged with making a decision on the dam project were alive the last time the government came a-knocking, the story of betrayal was passed along. For the Hopi it was as if the original bait-and-switch happened within weeks rather than decades. The Elders declined the government's request. It cost the government millions of dollars more because their plans had to be so radically changed.

To further this idea of generational time-keeping, while most western companies have a five-year plan (which changes every 30-seconds, it seems) a number of Japanese corporations have *100-year* business plans.

Whatever manner you track time, it is important. What we actually *do or don't do* within our time framework gives us a sense of satisfaction and fulfillment, or feelings of frustration and lost hope. We've all had that feeling of frustration when we didn't get something done by the time we had allotted. We've all felt the sensations of accomplishment when we completed something before it was due.

Time is critical. As a person with ADHD you must have a system that helps to keep you on-track. My personal system is a combination of a day-timer in which I block out times for production, meetings, etc. I also keep an Excel spreadsheet with my goals and tasks (my plan). But, if left to those two things, I will inevitably forget things. So, I also have a really big dry erase white-board in my office that lists the most current things I need to do. I use different colored markers for different types of tasks. I use a thick red marker to check things off the list when they are completed.

In talking to others with ADHD, having visual reminders is essential. Our brains are wired differently, and most with ADHD forget to do certain things. For example, I must keep my supplements and meds on the counter so I can see them. This visual cue helps me remember to take them. When they are put away…well, out of sight, out of mind. I forget to take them. Of course, I'll remember two hours later when I'm driving somewhere. I slap myself in the forehead and curse. And then laugh.

There is no one to blame for our inefficiencies. In knowing that we have ADHD, we understand that we can be prone toward distraction and forgetfulness. We must have a system. And, we must manage it. Sometimes we need help with that. While we are ultimately responsible for managing our system, having a support system is also important. Sometimes we do need people to remind us about important things like taking our meds or meeting a deadline.

There can be a propensity for people who support us to sometimes feel like they are babysitting us. That can happen. After all, "normal" people tend to manage their time better than we do, they remember to do things when they need to be done. They might think, *"If I can do this really simple thing, why can't you?"*

When it happens enough, and we hear that enough, that's when we start feeling like we're crazy. I know that's how I felt for a good portion of my life. Maybe you've felt that way, too. The thing is, the people who say these things to us are absolutely right…and they also don't understand.

It's up to you to educate them about ADHD and how you manifest it. It's also up to you to create a system to manage these things. The world *will not* adapt to you – you must adapt to it in order to be effective.

But, after you have introduced your system, and you have educated those around you about how ADHD manifests in your life, you can also ask them to help you. ***It is not babysitting!*** It is support.

In a perfect world you do not want to be forgetful or take twice as long to get something done. You are not lazy! You are not crazy! You are not stupid!

There is a reason why ADHD is considered an actual medical disorder. Less than 3% of the population is blessed with ADHD, and there are certain "dys-functional" ways our brains work. Our executive functions don't work the way "normal" executive brain functions work.

Put it this way, if a person is disabled and gets around in a wheelchair and has trouble making it up a steep hill, wouldn't you offer to help give them a push?

For those "normal" people – is this babysitting?

Of course not! The world may see us with ADHD as being lazy, crazy or stupid. It's yet another way in which people with mental health disorders are stigmatized. Unfortunately, it happens with us early on in school and can often follow us through the rest of our lives.

I say take things into your own hands and be responsible for your own "dis-order". Celebrate it. You are perfectly made by a perfect Creator. You have a purpose and plan in this life. And, to make perfect this plan, you need a system that includes people who exhibit understanding, are willing to give up judgment, and who don't consider themselves babysitters.

However, taking things into your hands means taking on everything. Being in relationship with someone who has ADHD is not easy. We have to accept this. We need to provide support to our supporters. Manage your system to the best of your ability. Demonstrate appreciation and gratitude. Be responsible for your eccentricities and the ways you create chaos (yes, you will still create chaos – though, hopefully, not nearly as much or as often as you once did). Never take for granted that being in relationship with you is always a joy-ride. It's not. ADHD, when left undiagnosed or unmanaged, can be hell on the people who live with you – and certainly you will suffer continuing consequences as well.

With all that being said, where do you begin with time?

Check your "sync". How do you and time relate?

Exercise #9: Are You In-Sync?

There's a difference between chronology and productivity - and each mark the passing of time. How do you mark time?

There is a lot to be said for running your own clock. While you may have made deadline agreements, all too often your relationship with time dictates when a project's completion date will be. But, in order to run your clock, you must also understand your relationship to time. When you alight on how your relationship to time works, you can begin planning your life much more effectively. If you have ADHD you must have this dialed-in. You must give yourself sufficient and appropriate time to get the work done.

What are your natural rhythms? Early to bed early to rise? Late to bed late to rise? Sleep in 2-4 hours slots at various times of the day?

Do you punch a clock or focus on productivity?

Do you compartmentalize or pepper divergent activities throughout your day?

Do you have a plan? How do you measure progress?

Do you feel like you spend your time wisely? If not, what do you need to change to make your investment into time more profitable and meaningful?

Make an assessment and find your time-buzz. Do this, and you'll find you'll not only get more done, but you'll accomplish those things that have meaning for you.

Once you understand your rhythms, what system will you use to keep track of to-do's and measure your productivity? This isn't just about work, either. It's about everything you do. Do you keep lists? Do you need visual cues? Do you need apps on your smart phone or iPad? Begin taking stock. Try different things. Once you get dialed in, put the system to use daily.

Part Two Summary

How are you mastering the basics? As you enter into your creative dreams, what are the essentials you need to understand? When you know what the basics are, do you practice them over and over again? For example, to master the art of writing songs, you might want to learn how to read and write music. When you do, practice the basics. Sit at your piano, pluck your harp, blow your horn – and get the basics *down*.

One tremendous technique for accumulating knowledge is to have an Individual Learning Plan. Using a basic 5-part structure, you can plan your learning. Do this – use the ILP – and you will continually acquire knowledge. A famous advertising executive once said that all creative genius begins with one thing – knowledge. So, get to learning!

If knowledge is your fuel, then your goal is the car you drive. Using the SMART goal setting system, you can separate wishes from actual goals. Use this process and you'll travel the right path – and get the results you want.

Become an apprentice. It works. Find the right person by going through the process outlined earlier in this chapter. Also create a super mentorship committee made from the great minds of history – learn about them and their lives. Imitate them. Pretend they are in the room with you, giving advice and encouragement.

Your environment is important. Make sure the physical environment pleases you and brings you comfort, and make sure there are people around you for honest support. You'll need it (we all do).

Understand your personal relationship with time. Create a workable and effective system for managing time, getting things done, and protecting your environment and process. Do not take this for granted. This is a must!

So, now you're equipped with knowledge. Keeping in mind that you will always quest for more knowledge, it's time to put your know-how to the test.

The Creative Process.

There is an absolute formula for creativity. Follow the path. Don't skip a step. The process is the doing…and what follows is how the process works. Understand the process and you can accomplish anything you set your mind to.

Part Three: The Creative Process

Our Connection to the Divine.

"Thinking is easy. Acting is difficult. To put one's thoughts into action is the most difficult thing in the world."
---Johann Wolfgang Von Goethe

"A creative man is motivated by the desire to achieve, not the desire to beat others."
---Ayn Rand

"I'm a very restless person. I'm always doing something. The creative process never really stops."
---Oscar de la Renta

"Don't worry about people stealing your ideas. If your ideas are any good, you'll have to ram them down people's throats."
---Howard Aiken

Giving Chaos Form.

The Hourglass

"Great indeed is the sublimity of the Creative to which all beings owe their beginning and which permeates all heaven."
   ---Lao Tzu

"Like sands in the hourglass, so are the days of our lives…"

Why is it that so many Creative Types live soap opera lives? Maybe it's the paparazzi world we live in, but it just seems like those we elevate as creative kings and queens always seem to fall from grace, find themselves in scandalous situations, or think their life is over if they do something that flops. It's the culture of the immediate, I suppose.

Of course, drama is par for the course for most with ADHD. Impulsivity control is a challenge for us – be it with our actions or our words. We've done and said things that seem totally crazy to others – but seemed like a good idea at the time to us (and, most of the time, they really weren't very good ideas). Bottom line – we do have a proclivity for creating drama and chaos. Often we do this to stimulate those parts of the brain that are deficient in the neurotransmitters needed to sustain "normalcy". The challenge for us is to channel our curiosity and impulsivity into productive activity.

I have a lot of respect for actor Robert Downey, Jr. From 1996 to 2001 his life was a train wreck. While he'd been nursing a drug addiction for some time, he began receiving bigger and bigger roles. And with each big role, his addiction became worse. The spiral reached its climax in 2000, when he was busted and spent time in court-ordered treatment compliments of the California Corrections system. At one point he told a judge that, *"It's like I have a loaded gun in my mouth and my finger's on the trigger…and I like the taste of gun-metal."*

He got busted again in 2001, made another appearance in the State's mandated drug treatment facility. His final arrest cost him his job on the TV series *Ally McBeal*, a role in the film *American Sweethearts*, and caused Mel Gibson's stage presentation of *Hamlet* to be shut down. He became uninsurable, unemployable…a Hollywood has-been.

But, after his 2001 rehab and a sentence of three years probation, he got clean.

He landed a few small gigs and then his close friend Mel Gibson actually paid for the excessive insurance financial backers now demanded whenever he was cast, and he appeared in *The Singing Detective*. Directors began to hire him (though in one instance, a producer withheld 40% of his salary until production wrapped as insurance against his history of addiction).

He landed a string of critically-acclaimed character roles in a number of films, and then was cast in his first blockbuster, *Iron Man*. With the huge success of that film, Downey's star once again shined.

Downey's rise and fall and rise again are part and parcel with the creative process.

The process itself is shaped like an hourglass. At the top of the hourglass is a vast horizon of chaos. This field of chaos is populated by broken things, problems of character, inefficient and outdated systems, products that don't work, a lack of beauty, boredom.

You get the picture.

Caught in a torrential flood – the sand whips and swirls like an industrial grinder against eroding river banks, tearing away nature. The nature of man is to create. If we don't, the world goes awry.

The Creative Type peers into the chaos and plucks a problem from the swirl. At that moment a thin stream of sand begins to pour into the top of the hourglass. This is the first step of taking chaos and giving it form and it's fueled by interest and desire. Next, the Creative Type begins whittling away, applying his or her unique blend of knowledge, skill and gut-instinct to give further form and definition.

The sand continues to pour, now more refined.

Challenges are encountered, and at times the Creative Type walks away, goes fishing, spends hours at Macy's, or rests in a hammock between swaying palms. And then lightning strikes. Inspiration, a gift from the divine. The Muse flutters in the breeze waiting to be captured again. The Creative Type is back at work now, applying her brilliance, and the challenge is overcome. Finally complete, the Creative Type then releases her creation to the world for its review, editing, rejection or acceptance.

And the creation no longer belongs to her.

As the world takes ownership of this new creation, the Creative Type snatches another handful of chaos from the horizon and starts the process again.

And so, truly, like sands in an hourglass, so are the days of our lives…

* * * * *

The Process always begins with a problem and our relationship to it. For the person with ADHD, it is important to be honest and realistic about the problems we encounter. However, as is often the case, our version of "honest and realistic" can be quite different than the way "normal" people may see the problem.

Remember, our brains are wired differently. We see the world through different eyes. How you see the world is the source of your uniqueness, your genius. You are perfectly made by a perfect Creator – and you are in this world for a reason. Your unique gifts are vital to the world around you, and maybe to the entire planet.

To enter the process we must be aware of this uniqueness. Unlike Robert Downey, or the host of others who have attempted to self-medicate through drugs, alcohol, shopping or sex, we mustn't try to "fix" ourselves. What we must do is prepare.

Preparation begins with a "cultural detox"…which then leads to chasing the Muse.

Getting Clear

The Cultural Detox

"Adventure must start with running away from home."
   —-William Bolitho

According to a recent study by the Kaiser Family Foundation, our kids (age 8-18) are packing in an average of nearly 11 hours of media *every day*. This is up just over 3 hours per day since 1999. So, how do they get all this media stuffed into their heads? Especially when they go to school, hang out with friends and still need 10 hours of sleep? Multi-tasking (a subject every person with ADHD understands intimately).

Imagine this: your 16 year old is writing a report at the family computer. As she's doing so, her ears are plugged into Brain Candy earphones attached to an iPod and there's a Hulu bug running in the lower left hand part of the computer screen. Of course, while she's typing away, she occasionally stops to do a Google search to discover some arcane fact about a disease you've never heard of, and while doing so her best friend sends her a text message. So, she goes to her Facebook page and adds her two-cents about the concert they'll be attending this weekend - and then returns to her report. Oh, and then she takes a selfie which she then Instagrams.

This is media multi-tasking.

Packing it all in. We used to call this sucking the marrow out of life. But, that was about experience. Today the experience is virtual. It's as if we're stuffed inside this digital pod and life is flashing all around us on high-def plasma screens. The brain doesn't discern what's "real" and what isn't. But, the body does.

Maybe that's why this generation of people under age 30 is so involved in adrenaline-pumping adventure sports like heli-skiing and base jumping.

All that adrenaline makes them feel alive. It's a cultural detox.

Granted, while they're leaping from the perfectly comfortable safety of a helicopter into the crystalline powder at 12,000 feet, they are plugged into their iPod's. And they're not listening to Beethoven. But, while the music is thumping on their frontal lobes, they are flushing the toxin of convention out of their bodies.

Music, movies, social networking sites, U-Tube, television, video games. This is the creative stuff they are consuming during most of their waking hours. Us older folk aren't too far away from this ourselves. Be it the computer, satellite radio, or television on our cell phones - we are bombarded by media every day as well.

And it can become overwhelming. Because, while we're consuming all that media, we typically aren't creating anything ourselves. Thus, we need to detox from news, sports, business, movies, politics and Facebook.

What does it take to detox? Depends on you. A walk through a forest. A day at the beach. Riding a bike along a lonely country road. Finding a quiet place to just sit for a while and observe nature. An evening of wine and laughter with friends. The detox can take many forms.

And then you're refreshed.
Instead of jumping back into media consumption, try your hand at creation. The benefits are phenomenal. Whether it's for business or pleasure, find an outlet for your creative impulses. As a creative being, if you don't give license to your impulse to create you'll just stuff it up inside, begin watching too much TV, and then decide to bungee jump off the Foresthill Bridge.

Trust me, there's just as much adrenaline pumping when you get in the zone creatively as there is in plummeting to your theoretical death from a safe and sound bridge. And, unlike the few seconds of air-time, being in the zone is a timeless thing that refreshes the soul. It's satisfying in a way that no risk-taking flight into the mouth of madness can simulate.

On the other hand, there's value in jumping off the bridge - and then writing about it.

Either way, in the media glutted world we exist within, the cultural detox is a necessary and valuable undertaking.

Even if it means jumping from a perfectly good bridge. This brings a clearing.

And it is in the clearing where the Muse will be found.

Chasing the Muse.

Since the beginning of time Creative Types have been chasing The Muse.

A source of inspiration, the mythical mystical creature takes her magic wand and taps us on the forehead one evening and, *voila*, the plot for a bestselling novel or an idea that will make us richer than Solomon in all his glory is suddenly at the forefront of our consciousness.

I wish it were that easy.

The Muse is playfully deceptive and sometimes cruel.

Yes, she comes unwarranted in the middle of the night (or when we're driving or taking a shower) and pings us with ideas. She drops hints, there are patterns, coincidence happens with frequency, we keep running into the same person, or we hear a song by the same artist 12 times in a day. If we keep missing her calling, sometimes she carts a sledgehammer and whacks us across the noggin.

However, ideas are pretty cheap. If you sat for a while and focused on any given subject, after an hour you'd have 50-100 ideas. As a Creative Type, you are an idea machine.

Of those 50-100 ideas, how many of them are *good* ideas? This, of course, is the challenge. Hanging your hat on a single idea is kind of scary - and yet, it must be done. This can be hard for someone with ADHD – we are a fountain flowing with ideas and we want to pursue every one of them.

Sometimes, especially in organizations, someone has the bright idea that 10 brains are better than one. If done correctly in a structured and focused manner, this can be a good method for solving problems. However, researchers at the University of Texas, Arlington have confirmed something that a lot of us already knew: brainstorming is B.S.

From a research stand-point, brainstorming is not only an inefficient means of generating ideas, but it may inadvertently chase away the Muse. Unfortunately, many people involved in brainstorming either get fixated on a single idea (and, thus, stop generating ideas in favor of the fixated one), or they engage in what's called "social loafing" - allowing others in the group to generate ideas while laggers mail it in. The process isn't democratic, either. Often one or two people can dominate while the rest of the group plays along passively. Or, a person in authority is present and not all ideas are put out on the table because they might be anti-authoritarian in nature or folk don't want their ideas rejected out of hand by the boss. Flat out, researchers have found that brainstorming is not the best way to generate ideas.

It will always come down to one motivated person—*you*.

Where do you find the Muse so you can chase her down? She's wherever you happen to look. The seeds for good ideas are all around you. They come at all hours of the day and night.

A good habit to take up is carrying a small journal with you wherever you go. When something pops into your mind or presents itself, just jot it down. The voice recorder in a cell phone can be used this way if you don't feel like carrying around a book.

When you get back to your home or office, flesh out the idea a little. You might want to keep an idea file on your computer, or keep one in a journal. Over time you will be amazed by the number of ideas you actually do generate.

Of course, that's when the real work starts. Once you chase down the Muse, you've gotta do something with her. The really cool thing about her is that when you fully commit to the creative process, she *will not* abandon you!

For now, get in the *habit* of paying attention to your thoughts and your environment. Get in the *habit* of writing things down.

Ideas are the DNA of creativity. As someone with ADHD, you are an idea machine! So what do you do with all of those brilliant *a-ha's*? You need to catch them...

Creative DNA

Catching Lightning in a Bottle

"Bruce Lee was an artist and, like him, I try to go beyond the fundamentals of my sport. I want the public to see a knockout in the making."
—-Sugar Ray Leonard

"The good parts of a book may be the only something a writer is lucky enough to overhear or it may be the wreck of his whole damn life – and one is as good as the other"
   ---Ernest Hemmingway

Inspiration is a strange thing.

It comes at the oddest times and in the strangest places. It's like lightning. It strikes and we stand back in awe and wonder and say, *"Wow, isn't that beautiful, exciting and scary?"* Or, *"Jeez, glad I wasn't standing under a tree when that thing hit."*

Ideas are like that, too. Great ideas are beautiful, exciting and scary. Anything innovative and new, something that takes us out of our comfort zones, will generate excitement... and fear. This is normal.

The exciting and scary part comes when we **take action** on the idea. That's catching lightning in a bottle. The moment we act on the idea, we have a responsibility to see it through to a logical conclusion.

Sometimes that means taking it all the way to completion. Finishing the painting. Launching a new product. Planting a new garden. Implementing a new policy. Writing a novel.

But, sometimes it also means stopping. That's right, *stopping*.

I have at least half a dozen unfinished novels in my file cabinet. Either I lost interest, or I determined I wasn't the person to write this particular story, or I needed to let the thing simmer and incubate. I'm okay with letting them sit. The lightning may strike again. Or it won't. That's fine. **There's always another idea to take its place**.

On the other hand...

Have you ever had a great idea that you just sat on - only to discover later that the *same* idea was acted upon by another person? And now they're rolling in dough or became famous? We've all experienced this once or twice.

Once the lousy feelings pass, don't beat yourself up. You obviously weren't the right person for *that* idea. It was someone else's calling. So, sometimes releasing the lightning is a good thing.

I believe in Jung's concept that there is a collective consciousness. Ideas swirl around the cosmos awaiting the right person to pluck one out. For that reason, ideas are actually pretty cheap. They don't require a lot from us. It's **commitment** to the idea that has its cost.

Unfortunately, sometimes it's *not* that we're the wrong person. We just don't act. That's when creative regret will come knocking on your door.

What's sad is that the idea was never given an opportunity to live and breathe. What's worse, by not taking some kind of action, *you deny yourself the opportunity of discovery* - one of the great joys in being alive.

Avoid the regret of dead dreams. Process the idea fully.

Give the idea a chance to fly on its own by taking this approach when the Muse pays a visit:

#1. *Quickly sketch out the idea*. Put pen to paper (or fingers to keyboard) and describe it. Provide as much detail as possible, and construct it in its finished form to the best of your ability.

#2. *Imagine it fully*. How does the idea feel? Taste? Smell? What's it look like? And, if it's for the benefit of others, how do they respond emotionally? What are its benefits? How do *you* feel about it? Are the rewards internal, external or both? Don't fret if you don't have all the answers - just *imagine*.

#3. *Reign in fear and doubt*. Pretend the thought police are eating donuts on a street corner in Joliet, IL. They're nowhere around. Give yourself full permission to experience the feelings, without editing. Fear and doubt is the two-headed Grim Reaper of dead dreams. Don't give him entry into your thoughts!

#4. *Let it simmer*. Unless you can begin work on it *right now*, let it simmer for a day or two. Come back to it with a fresh mind and begin working it. If the passion is still there, go for it.

#5. *Play it out*. Keep working on it. If it's meant to be, passion will transform into commitment. It's the commitment that will fuel you when passion wanes.

Or...

#6. *Let it go*. If your interest wanes, let it go for a while. Don't force it. If you come back to it later and the fire returns, keep working. But, if the fire is more like a sputtering match-head, move on. Don't try to fit a square peg into a round hole.

#7. *Whatever happens, let it be okay*. And don't beat yourself up. You gave the idea a chance to germinate. Maybe it's just not time for it yet, or you simply are not the right person to give it full life.

I can recall many times when I plucked a half-completed article from my hopper and finished it. It may have been sitting there for three years. It was time for it to be born. So, don't sweat it if the lightning fizzles.

And keep in mind that lightning *always* strikes again - but, just in different places.

The Personal Slush Pile

"If at first the idea is not absurd, then there is no hope for it."
—-**Albert Einstein**

Do you have a slush pile?

You know, a file cabinet filled with unfinished projects? I do. And I'm glad I have one. Now, as a person with ADHD, I'm bound to have a million unfinished projects, right?

While suffering through a flu-bug that kicked the tar out of me a while back, I woke up in the middle of night, unable to breathe, and re-imagined a novel I wrote 15 years ago.

It must have come out of a sleep-deprived haze of sinus muck and aching joints, but I suddenly remembered this book. Back when I actually had energy to spare I wrote a number of novels that, after a few half-hearted attempts to publish, got tossed into the slush bin.

Since I never throw away anything I've written - even the bad high school poetry - my labors of love have shared space with a dozen other novels and books that, for whatever reason, I lost interest in completing.

Either the idea just petered out, or I had a good idea that wasn't ready to emerge, or maybe my writing was terrible and I couldn't take the masochistic experiment anymore. Whatever the reason, these projects needed to age gracefully or just die.

This book I resurrected, though, has never really left me. I actually completed this one. But, when I finished it, I knew that it could be better. So, I set it aside believing I'd get back to it within a couple of weeks. Life, of course, had a different design.

So, it's been 15 years. And it's a good thing. The basic plot has remained the same, but as I began to write, the characters have emerged with more depth and my narrative style has changed substantially. After writing the first page or two, I knew this book would be better, and would take on a different life.

So, once I felt a little better, I experienced a complete period of flow and wrote five chapters in four days. I came to a roadblock and let the thing simmer. But, I know where the story is going.

I'll finish this one. It's just got that feel, that vibe, and it's getting close. When it's done it will be published, either by someone else or by me. The options 15 years ago weren't nearly as plentiful as today. But, that's a completely different process. For now, I'm just enjoying this period of hopped-up creativity.

So, do you have a slush pile? If you don't, start one. It's easy. Print out all the unfinished stuff you've got stored in your hard drive. Go through your boxes of handwritten notes, creative ideas and otherwise incomplete projects. Clean out a drawer in one of your filing cabinets and stuff it with all that unfinished work.

As you put your stuff in the file, you'll naturally begin reading your half-completed masterpieces. I predict you'll find a jewel or two that you'll set aside and begin re-working. Maybe it's a sketch you made on a napkin while waiting for your date. Perhaps it's the outline of a brilliant marketing campaign that just never found its legs. Could be the first ten pages of a screenplay that just lost steam.

Maybe you'll take that sketch and re-work it into a painting you'll hang in your study. The marketing campaign - a new product. The screenplay? Perhaps it'll become the basis of the novel you've always wanted to write.

The slush pile has immense value because great ideas have a long shelf-life. They exist so long as you keep them handy.

(Note: As mentioned earlier, as a person with ADHD, your slush pile is a valuable resource. It is not, however, an excuse to never finish anything. So a note of caution: only go to the slush pile when you really need a new thought, a forgotten jewel, or you're in-between projects. Don't let it be a source of rabbit-trailing. Get your work done!).

Quit talking. Start doing. Taking action.

Writers *Write*

"In spite of your fear, do what you have to do."
—-Chin Ning Chu

"If you don't take risks, you won't achieve anything."
---Sir Richard Branson

Painters paint, leaders lead and firemen put out fires. If you want to be something, you need to do it.

I have met a countless number of people who have said to me, "I love to write (or, I want to write), but I never find the time." That's fine. But, I begin thinking of the countless number of dreams that are going unfulfilled. In fact, every day that goes by that those people don't do the things that would bring them real joy, two things simultaneously happen

First, I think they incrementally lose touch with their souls. Whether they were meant to write (or paint, or start a business, or whatever), another seed of dissatisfaction with their life is planted. Over time these seeds take root and it becomes harder and harder for them to get rid of these life-choking weeds. The life of quiet desperation simply becomes a part of their identity and they are lost to obligation, expectation and resignation. It's pretty sad.

Maybe they were never meant to be a great artist or business-person, but, how would they know if they never tried?

And, second, they deny the world the gift of their talents. While they may not discover a cure for cancer, if someone always wanted to go to medical school and become a doctor, but instead settled for a life working as a bookkeeper or a road worker, all of the people they might have helped heal will never know the uniqueness of their special gifts. By not doing what was needed to go to medical school (or even go into some other healing profession), they commit theft by omission.

Unfortunately, so many of these would-be's either think they don't have what it takes and don't have the self-confidence to pursue their dreams; think they lack the necessary resources; or someone has told them to play it safe and take the "secure" route. And every one of these is an excuse they've come to believe. Flat out, these are lies.

Here's the truth: you *do* have what it takes to pursue your dreams; every resource you need is at-hand (you just may have to dig a little deeper); and playing it safe is *never* secure.

It reminds me of a football team that is leading the game in the 4th quarter. Instead of continuing to do the things that put them into the lead, they play it safe, run "prevent" defenses, and quit taking even the smallest risk. Invariably, the other team will score. "Prevent" defenses are just another way of giving into fear – and it *always* leads to under-achievement or flat-out failure. While someone may play it safe in order to avoid rejection, they miss multiple opportunities to make their lives and the lives of others happier.

Writers write. Pretty simple.

Even if it's just 15 minutes a day. Scott Turow was a practicing attorney who wrote his bestselling novel, *Presumed Innocent*, while riding the subway to work everyday. J.K. Rowling wrote Harry Potter while sitting in a coffee shop. A friend of mine, Carey, was a football coach who was always called to become a marriage and family therapist. He went to night school and found a non-traditional masters program. It took him a while, but today he has his own counseling practice. And he's happy.

So, what's your dream?

Are you willing to take at least one step a day toward fulfilling it – even if it's just making a phone call or writing long-hand at the kitchen table 15 minutes a day?

I promise this – if you do commit, and take just one step each day, after a while something magical happens. You find more time to do what you love. The lack of confidence falls away and you simply do what you do because you're finding immense joy – and you want that joy daily. Your life takes on a different flavor. You're happier, and it shows.

What's your first step? Write it down. Do it today. Tomorrow, write down the next step – and keep doing this until your dream becomes an action you take daily. Not because you *have* to – but, because you *must*. Not doing it becomes like forgetting how to breathe.

It's just something you do – because writers *write*.

The Flame that Burns Brightest of All.

"Desire is the starting point of all achievement, not a hope, not a wish, but a keen pulsating desire which transcends everything."
   ---Napoleon Hill

Some will call it the "burning in the belly". Others call it the "internal fire". It's the fuel that keeps you moving forward regardless of the price to be paid. It's the quality that pushes you through fear, helps you over-come challenges, and pulls you through the tough times.

Desire.

This isn't something that can be learned or taught. Desire comes from inside of you. You either have it or you don't. But, sometimes desire can be an elusive thing to identify.

It's kind of like romance. Let's say you meet a wonderful person who just might be "The One". You date for a while and all seems to be going great – you're in the romantic phase, after all. What you're feeling inside (the butterflies in the stomach whenever he's near; heart-pounding joy when she puts her hand in yours) definitely feels like the real thing.

But, is it?

Infatuation can feel a lot like love, most certainly. And, most love experts will say that the early romantic phase is just that – infatuation. Everything is right with the world. Your special person has no blemishes; she is perfect in every way; he walks on water.

That is, until he or she forgets an important date, or says something hurtful, or blows you off for an evening with his friends.

Love works through the hard stuff, while infatuation dims quickly when confrontation and conflict come to pay a visit.

The same holds true for the creative process. As a Creative-Type, it is very likely you have many varied interests. Something bright and shiny and new will capture your fancy and you may spend a few days, a week, even a month or so having fun with it. Just when you think you've found your true ultimate calling, something else crosses your path and you're off to the races again. As a person with ADHD, you probably know all about this.

Your infatuation with the shiny thing wasn't your calling after all. It also wasn't a waste of time – after all, you likely acquired new knowledge of some type.

Creative or intellectual infatuations are like that. For example, I'm kind of a space buff. I really enjoy the mind-expanding discussions of quantum and theoretical physics as they relate to the exploration of space. I'm very interested – but, is it my calling?

No. Too much math.

Desire becomes attached to those one or two things that make you go into psychosocialcreative withdrawal. Go too long without playing in the sandbox with your favorite toys and you become an irritable, grouchy, unpleasant person who begins to eat or drink too much, watch too much

TV, or hang out at the mall beyond what's good for you or your wallet.

When you finally hunker down and embrace your true love, you get the rush. Everything around you is shut out. Time literally stops for you. You're truly happy.

That's desire. It is a necessary element in the creative equation. While you can't truly explain *why* you feel this level of joy when you're doing your thing, nevertheless, you experience it. Like love, it's a wonderful mystery.

Exercise #10: Fire in the belly.

What is that *one thing* that, if you didn't do it, your life would feel incomplete?

Make it into a statement. For example:

"If I didn't write in my journal everyday I would go stark, raving mad! I will not compromise, deal away or give up writing in my journal daily for anyone or anything. Period."

Identify it. Make a statement. Be faithful to this statement.

And then do the next indicated thing: focus your attention.

Focus

The Benefit of Focus: When Work is Play.

"Your work is to discover your work and then with all your heart give yourself to it.
—-Buddha

"Play has been man's most useful pre-occupation."
—-Frank Caplan

Every one of us has heard the advice, "Do what you love and the rewards will follow." This advice is on the money and kind of obvious, right?

Of course it is. But, it doesn't mean, "Do what you love and *get paid well* for it." That's a different horse of a very peculiar color. The fact is, most people do not get paid for what they love to do—and this is where we get hung up.

Study after study consistently indicates that only 25% of workers are actively enrolled and engaged in what they do. Studies also show that at any given time, approximately 50% of those employed are looking for a new job.

We are multi-faceted beings with numerous interests, obligations and responsibilities in every area of life. Some things - like doing taxes - are chores that we may not like, but have to get done. This comes with the territory of daily living.

Dan Brown, the author of the mega-bestseller *DaVinci Code* said, *"I hate to write, but love to have written."*

This attitude isn't uncommon. After all, we're addicted to outcomes. This isn't wrong or bad—in fact, results *do* matter. But, the over-emphasis on outcomes can end up killing the joy of the process. With any creative endeavor, *the process is an outcome in itself.*

When we commit to the process - the actual doing of something - and we find ourselves becoming lost in it like a wonderful dream, something magical happens.

We experience happiness. We experience fulfillment. We experience deep competency - an inward feeling of mastery, oneness and joy.

There is pure joy in a perfecting a brushstroke, delivering an eloquent and heart-felt speech, hitting notes that were always out of reach, acquiring a new account. Satisfaction comes from living inside the moments of creation - overcoming a difficult challenge, finally mastering a skill after years of practice, throwing the perfect pitch at the right moment. Within the process we experience the flow of life.

Happiness is a state of being, not a destination. It comes from doing the things we love doing - activities that bring forth the depth of our uniqueness and provide a means for authentic expression of our most deeply held values.

Does this mean you have to undertake a series of epic projects? No. It just means making a connection with your values in everything you do - and investing your time in doing those things that bring you pleasure.

Focusing on what you love is not a selfish pursuit.

It makes you a happier and more balanced human being. By making ***"Do what I love"*** a core value, you might find that, while the challenges of life may not be easier, it makes the journey a lot less hazardous. The more you apply this value to what you do for a living, you enter into that place where work becomes like play. Yes, there will still be the stuff you don't want to do, but because your attitude has shifted, you'll get through that stuff faster so you can get on to what you find enjoyable.

But, your work isn't necessarily what you do for a living. Hopefully your 9 to 5 is spent doing meaningful, productive and enjoyable activities - but, even if you're just doing it for the paycheck (which is not a dishonorable thing at all), you can be defined by other expressions that bring you joy.

My grandfather, Herb, comes to mind. He left his home in Canada for the U.S. when he was 16. It was dust-bowl and depression time, so he rode the rails, did odd jobs, and finally landed in California, where he went to work operating a carousel at a boardwalk amusement park in Oceanside. That's where he met the love of his life, my grandmother, Babe.

It wasn't long before they headed to Yuma, AZ and got married. The wedding ring he gave her cost $29 - and she wore that ring until the day she died - nearly 70 years later. They moved to Los Angeles, started a family, and Herb went to work for a bakery, and then later, became a parts-man for a car dealership in Anaheim.

Herb worked hard. He received a number of accommodations for service excellence while at the Chevrolet dealership - and he never made more than $1,000 per month. But, Herb loved what he did. He was good at it. He taught himself about auto parts and managing an efficient inventory system. He used many of his natural gifts. People liked his quick, dry wit and his attention to detail. He lived his values. He *always* gave an honest day's work for an honest day's pay. That's a big part of what defined him.

What also fueled his spirit, though, were non-job related activities. He and Babe lived in an old farmhouse on 2 acres of land on the outskirts of Anaheim, scrunched between a strawberry patch and an orange grove. As their three children grew older, they joined 4-H and began raising animals: goats, chickens, pigs, rabbits. Herb and Babe became involved as 4-H leaders, taking a hands-on approach in assisting numerous children learn and appreciate the value of agriculture, hard work and building solid character. It was their passion until their youngest daughter, Patty, graduated from high school. While they became involved because of their own children, their tireless commitment to all of the kids benefited everyone in their local culture.

The second passion was bowling. Herb was a small, wiry man - no more than 5'6" 135 pounds, but he sure knew how to knock down pins. Participating in mixed leagues with Babe, and men's leagues with his son and son-in-law, Herb stoked his competitive fires at Highland Lanes in Fullerton, CA every Wednesday and Friday night. He certainly wasn't the best or worst on the lanes, but he never missed a game and always put everything he had into every roll.

Bowling and being a 4-H leader. On the surface most wouldn't necessarily consider these things creative-activities. But, below the surface there was a lot going on.

In both activities, Herb was a leader. He applied his time, energy, intellect and effort into learning all he could about being the best leader he could be. While he wasn't standing at a podium inspiring millions, what he did sure had meaning to all of the children that he led in 4-H, and to the many bowling teammates he had over the years. They came to rely upon him and respect him for his commitment.

In each endeavor he had to learn new skills and acquire new knowledge. After all, this was a poor kid who left home at 16 after his parents died. He wasn't blessed with a college education, nor was he well-connected or was privy to a trust fund. He had to make his own way, and he did so through sheer grit and determination.

His values aided him greatly in being married to Babe for 61 years, and raising three children, all of whom went on to enjoy successful careers and raise families of their own. For Herb, raising his family, earning a living, focusing on the needs of others, and taking time to have a little fun gave him a balance that epitomizes success. Because of the era and culture he was born into, security was important. But, what he learned was that his endless commitment to learning was where his *real* security would spring – a value held by true Creative Types.

Herb was never perceived as being selfish for doing those things he loved because in expressing his authentic self he naturally benefited others.

Herb's life demonstrates how work can actually feel like play. Like breathing, it's just something you do, a part of who you are, and cause for experiencing happiness.

That's the point. Making work seem like play is a simple combination of investing time in what brings you pleasure, and changing your attitude about those things that don't.

For an example, unlike Dan Brown, I enjoy the process of writing. Is it hard work sometimes? Yes, it is. But I find fulfillment through that work, even on those days when what I put down on paper isn't very good. Outcome doesn't matter at that point - the process will eventually take care of the outcome, and it does. In the end, the writing is better and my audience, whether it's a corporate CEO or those reading my books, or anyone else taking time to read my stuff, receive more value and benefit from the work.

For me, that's what making work into play is all about. Letting go of the outcome long enough to enjoy the ride. And, hopefully, others will benefit from the work.

Herb enjoyed the ride. So can you. And one of the key ingredients is focus.

Digging the Best Ditch Ever

"Genius is one per-cent inspiration and 99 per-cent perspiration."
---Thomas Alva Edison

Have you ever dug a ditch? Were you filled with enthusiasm and excitement while you were shoveling away the dirt?

In all likelihood, you just wanted the job to be done. After all, digging ditches for most people just doesn't fire the heart with joy and sublime feelings of creative genius.

However, consider the Erie Canal. When it was completed in 1825 it was often called the 8th Wonder of the World. It included 18 aqueducts to carry water over ravines and rivers, and 83 locks with a rise of 568 feet from the Hudson River to Lake Erie. It was 4 feet deep and 40 feet wide, and could easily accommodate boats carrying 30 tons of freight.

The idea for the canal had been floated as early as 1768, but the New York State Legislature didn't fund a survey for the project until 1808. It finally broke ground in 1817. Many at the time considered it sheer lunacy, and often referred to it as "Clinton's Big Ditch". You see, New York Governor DeWitt Clinton had a vision of connecting New York with the Great Lakes in the upper Midwest, thereby creating a commerce thoroughfare that nothing but the mighty Mississippi River could parallel. The difference, of course, is that the Eerie Canal was a feat of human engineering. And it required a massive amount of focus.

The primary skill required in dream accomplishment is focus. How well you focus will determine the depth and quality of your achievement.

"The focus and the concentration and the attention to detail that flying takes is a kind of meditation. I find it restful and engaging and other things slip away."
—-**Harrison Ford** (On being a pilot)

Concentrating one's focus is of paramount importance. All things being equal, the ability to focus your attention on one thing at a time is a skill that every successful Creative Type possesses. The reasons are kind of obvious.

Have you ever tried to get something done but kept being interrupted? Did you find that you never quite found the "flow"? You might be surprised at how costly interruptions and the lack of consistent focused attention can be.

According to a survey done by BaseX, *The Cost of Not paying Attention: How Interruptions Impact Knowledge Worker Productivity*, interruptions of attention cost U.S. business $588 *billion* per year in lost productivity. The survey also shows that 28% of a worker's day is consumed by interruptions.

Other surveys show that people are now working longer hours at the office, and are taking work home more and more. All this despite the promise that technology would actually make work easier, more efficient, and would lead to far greater balance. *Yeah, right.*

Technology has actually *added* to the interruption/distraction factor. The internet, e-mail, cell phones, text messaging, Twitter, U-Tube and Facebook consume an inordinate amount of our time. We need to get a handle on this. Especially if you have ADHD!

On-the-job we're also dealing with all kinds of personal interruptions from supervisors, subordinates, colleagues and friends. At home it could be children, pets, phone calls from friends, phone calls from telemarketers, television and the computer.

Our collective attention is being assaulted not on a daily basis, but on a *minute-by-minute* basis. We don't seem to have the luxury of just 10-minutes of concentrated focus.

But, if concentrated focus is what true, quality, lasting achievement requires, what can we do? Especially if we have ADHD?

You must learn to guard your focus by considering your attention to be something sacred - as if it were a precious and rare gem. There is no other way.

It *is* sacred. Think about it this way. Life is something that is experienced. The only conduit for experience is through our attention. If our attention is constantly shattered, fragmented and cut short, our experience of life will reflect this fragmentation.

Fragmentation gives birth to negative stress - which, of course, zaps our productivity, energy and joy. If sustained, it can also lead to all kinds of terrible health consequences like heart disease, hypertension and high blood pressure.

Given these consequences, don't you think guarding your focus and attention is kind of a good thing?

Of course it is. While you won't be able to shut-off all of the interruptions that come your way - and some interruptions are absolutely necessary (i.e. the baby needs to be fed, the big boss has an urgent task that only you can do, etc.), you can erect a series of strong boundaries that will protect your most valuable resource - your attention.

#1. Tune-off. According to Nielsen, the average person watches 142 hours of television each month (that's a total of 6 full days!). What could you accomplish if you cut your TV consumption in half?

#2. Click-off. Depending on age, we spend 14-20 hours per week online. Facebook may be important, but is the time you spend chatting about what you watched on TV last night more important than your dreams? What if you cut *that* time in half? You'd gain a full work day per week!

#3. The 10-4 principle. Okay, maybe you *do* need to keep the computer on all day for work. The worst attention-stealing bandit is e-mail. It's real easy to become addicted to checking your in-box 12 times an hour. I've been there. However, with a little discipline, you can reduce your total time doing e-mail to about 20 minutes per day. Make a habit of checking your in-box at 10am and 4pm. And that's it. Most people who use this system say that whatever came through between 10:10 and 4:00 isn't urgent, and can wait. To make things even more efficient, many e-mail programs have a filter through which e-mails of certain subjects are funneled into designated folders. This means that instead of dealing with 50 e-mails, you may only need to look at 2 or 3.

#4. The purpose of a door. Is to open and close. We'll emphasize *closed* here. Beyond leaving the premises, a closed door is the most effective interruption barrier known to man. What makes it even more effective is if you put a little sign on the outside of the door that says, "Please do not disturb if door is closed." You'll only be disturbed for two reasons: 1) There's an emergency, or, 2) A really obnoxious narcissist who believes you must talk to him is at the other end of the knock (if they knock). Respect the first reason, and you have permission to shoot the other one (a bent paper-clip and rubber band work really well). Just remember, in an office scenario, an open door is also an open invitation. Empower yourself. Close the door.

#5. Silence is golden. Most office phones are equipped with a Do-Not-Disturb button. Learn to use it - especially when you've closed your door.

#6. Silence is golden 2.0. This includes cell phones. Switch to "silent" or "meeting" mode. Or, better yet, just turn the darned thing off. Same goes for pagers, PDA's and any other gadget that people can use to interrupt your flow.

#7. Quit chasing rabbits. "Rabbit trailing" happens when you go to do one thing, and end up having your attention diverted and doing something else. This happens a lot with e-mail - but it also can occur when you're going through a file, sorting your mail or sifting through a stack of newsletters. If something catches your interest, stick it in another pile and get to it after you've completed your main task.

#8. Leave. Whether you're at work or at home, if it's just one of those days in which everyone and everything is getting in the way and slicing away your concentration - go somewhere else. Find a vacant office on another floor. Go to an unused conference room. There's usually an internet café somewhere close by. Just go. Heck, even McDonald's has WiFi now. Go get a McFrappe's and enjoy the aroma of French fries cooking and Big Mac's sizzling.

#9 Declare your freedom. The workplace is actually easier to declare boundaries than at home. After all, everyone in your office faces the same interruptions you do. If you mark your boundaries colleagues may follow suit and, who knows, your office may win a productivity award led by your example. But, it's at home where the trouble lies. Family members—especially children and husbands - don't get it. So, you have to make them get-it. With gentleness and love, let your family know that you are unequivocally and irrevocably unavailable from 7 to 9 every Saturday morning (or whenever is best). Let them know that you appreciate their respect and support. Eventually one of your loving family members will crash your boundary. The first time that happens, in a gentle and loving voice, let them know that the next time your boundary is disrespected there will be consequences. Dream these penalties up before the transgression so you can let them know specifically what will happen. If you're the cook of the house, let them know they are on their own (or your spouse/SO is now the cook) for the next day. Make them do their own laundry. If a child is the crasher, let them know that because they interrupted you and disrespected your time, you now don't have time to take them to the mall. This strategy works. Use it. For more back-up on this, check out *Parenting Teens with Love and Logic* by Foster and Fay. It's a great book with excellent strategies that work on kids, teens and errant adults.

#10. Take your meds. Remember your brain and how it fires differently? Well, if your ADHD has been diagnosed, then you also have a protocol for ensuring that you have the right amounts of chemicals getting fired and frontal lobe blood flow. Maybe you have a prescription for Adderall or another drug. If so, take it. Maybe you have a natural approach involving supplements, take them, too.

#11. Reward yourself. Yes, accomplishment is its own reward. But, giving yourself that new gadget you want or a double fudge sundae is also kind of nice. Reward your diligence and adherence to investing your focus. The bigger the accomplishment, the more grand the reward. And, if you did this at home and your family supported you, spread the wealth. Do something fun as a family. If at work, and you had team members support you, send them a hand-written thank-you note offering sincere appreciation. Getting others in on your action is a good thing. They'll respect you and your time more and more.

Speaking of rewards...remember the Eerie Canal? Governor Clinton's unceasing focus on his "Big Ditch" led to New York City becoming the most prosperous city in the world. Focused attention absolutely has its rewards.

That being said, there will come a time in the process when, no matter how hard you focus, the answer will not come. When this occurs, it's time to simmer.

Simmering

Sometimes Playing Hooky is the Only Option

"If you obey all the rules you miss all the fun."
—-**Katherine Hepburn**

I know the rules.

Write something every day. Be disciplined. Obey the routine. I know.
This stuff is true. When I work on a big project, like a novel, writing
daily is essential. Momentum matters, even when all I'm writing is crap.
Every now and then, though, you just need to take a break.

I made that choice after taking my daughter to the Treasure Island Music
Festival. It wasn't so much the Festival, but all the time I had to think
about stuff while I was wandering around feeling self-conscious in my
electric blue Polo hoodie while all the kids were wearing Black. They
were having so much fun and I was thinking about all my problems. As I
watched them dancing in the grass to music I'd never heard before, I decided to take a break.

The break lasted 10 days.

It was good incubation time. And, as far as the creative process is concerned, incubation is an essential phase. While we often just think about

stuff like art, writing, business and romance in creative terms, our *entire lives are a creative process*. Every moment we breathe is a creating moment.

I know. It's getting kind of woo-woo in here. But, whether it feels a little squishy or not, it's still true.

So, since your life is a creative process, don't be afraid or feel guilty to take a break.

Take a metaphoric (or literal) walk in the park and get some fresh air. You might be surprised how much it helps.

Just know that incubation is also a part of the process.

The Value of Incubation

"One should never impose one's views on a problem; one should rather study it, and in time a solution will reveal itself."
  ——-**Albert Einstein**

"No wine before its time."

It's a line from an old television commercial with Orson Welles presenting the value of incubation. The idea is that good things often take time to develop - that a great idea must have sufficient time to incubate before given life in the world.

Incubation isn't to be confused with inaction. Quite the contrary. In fact, over the course of a project, there may be several periods of pulling away and letting the thing simmer in its juices. Kind of like removing a really good steak from the grill and letting it sit for a few minutes. It continues to cook while the juices settle in, tenderizing, flavoring and perfecting.

When vexed by a problem, Albert Einstein would often speak the problem into his subconscious just before retiring to bed. During his sleep the problem would often be resolved and he'd awaken with a solution. Norman Maclean didn't publish *A River Runs Through It* until he was in his 70's. That book took a lifetime to incubate.

Great ideas just take time. The key factor involved with incubation is completely letting go for a while. We'll often throw all of our psychic, emotional and physical energies into a project. Inevitably we'll come to a roadblock or a fork in the road. Unless we have clear direction in which way to proceed, it becomes time to incubate.

Walk away. Go fishing. Read poetry. Play with your children or grand-children. Do something relaxing that takes your mind away from the challenge. And, no matter what, don't return to it until you have *"the moment"*.

The Moment **often comes at a really inopportune time**. It comes while you're driving, or you're in the shower, or you're engaged in an activity that is as far removed from the project as possible. In a flash of super-charged neurotransmitted energy, **the ANSWER comes**. It's clear, decisive and distinct. You *know* it's the solution.

When you give the challenge a chance to roll around in your subconscious and incubate, the deep recesses of your mind never stop working on the problem. It just needs time and *unencumbered space* to work the thing out. That's how the process works - so, let the process serve you. Next time you run into a brick wall and you don't know how you'll go through it, around it or over it, let it go. And let it simmer.

However, there is a distinction here that someone with ADHD must adhere to: when you walk away, DO NOT, UNDER ANY CIRCUMSTANCE, START A NEW PROJECT!

Incubation is a valuable and necessary part of the creative process. When you walk away, whether for an hour or a week, you are giving your conscious mind a chance to rest. But, your subconscious is hard at work.

Starting a new project undermines this process!

If you are in a work scenario, in which you have several projects going at one time, make an attempt to come back to the project in question from time to time. This takes discipline. The advice here, though, is to not *start* another major project until your answer comes. Typically in a work environment you are on a deadline. The combination of incubation and a deadline stimulates creative tension, which will actually speed the incubation process.

Don't worry. Trust the process. The answer you seek is coming.

In the meantime, while you're stopping to smell the roses and your sub-conscious is hammering out solutions, another important thing is happening.

You're becoming refreshed. Energy is being restored.

Let the Power Flow

"I could not, at any age, be content to sit in the corner and look on."
—**Eleanor Roosevelt**

There has always been some controversy as to which periods of life we find ourselves to be most creative. Like so much in life, it depends.

The proliferation of technology has blurred this historical reality, though. Stories of techno wizardry from 20-somethings abound. Larry Page and Sergey Brin started Google when they were grad students at Stanford during the late 1990's. Bill Gates dropped out of college and started Microsoft. During his mid-20's, Steve Wozniak invented the Apple computer and launched Apple with Steve Jobs and Ronald Wayne.

The work of these men, all in their 20's, has changed our cultural landscape forever. There is no doubt about that. And, maybe for this reason, we assign the 20's as our most productive and creative age.

But, that's not really true. In his seminal work on creativity, *Creativity: Flow and the Psychology of Discovery and Invention*, Mihaly Csikszent-mihalyi, studied the lives of 94 prominent people who, in his estimation, had contributed significantly to the culture. All of the people interviewed were over the age of 60. After all, he was looking at a lifetime of work. Today I am certain that people like Wozniak and Gates would be included in his sampling. After all, even up to his early death, Steve Jobs was continually creating and innovating.

Significant creative output, based on this study, may be more tied to one's field or domain. Without getting too bogged down in study-speak the bottom-line is this: creative output is a lifetime gig.

Frank Lloyd Wright designed the Guggenheim when he was 91. Michaelangelo was painting the Pauline Chapel at the Vatican when he was 89. Linus Pauling says he published twice as many papers after 70 than he did during his "productive" years. Benjamin Franklin invented bi-focals when he was 78. Novelists often don't publish their first book until they are in their 40's.

It depends on the field and the person. It's true that mathematicians often do their best work during their 20's and 30's, as do many physicists. However, while Albert Einstein formed the basis of his Theory of Relativity at age 26, he continued working on the questions of quantum mechanics up until his death at age 76.

I think it comes down to this: when we're young, we have a lot of energy but little experience. As we age, this begins to reverse. For example, at this point in my life I still have a lot of ideas, but not nearly the energy I had when I was 25. So, at this point, what matters most is the *quality* of output.

But, output still needs energy. What do we need to do to capture the energy needed to make a contribution? Here are some ways (not that any of them are all that new - you've heard this stuff before):

Get enough sleep. Sleep deprivation has all kinds of serious mental and physical consequences. We all need between 6-8 hours of sleep each night. That's when our brains process all the information we've encountered during the course of a day, storing everything in its proper place - including memories. After getting enough sleep, we awake fresh and ready to gather more information and we have the energy to do the stuff that's important to us. When we don't get enough sleep, we create a "sleep debt" - eventually all that lost sleep must be re-paid to the brain. Our body has natural rhythms. When we lose sleep, these rhythms get screwed up. The more sleep deprived we become, the less effective we are. We all know this is true. For everything you ever wanted to know about sleep, check out the National Sleep Foundation's website (sleepfoundation.org).

Eat healthy stuff. This is a no-brainer. But, those fudge covered Oreos are just too tempting, right? Well, yes, they are. Keep in mind, though, that sugar (especially for someone with ADHD) can substantially limit brain-power. A good mix of proteins and carbs are necessary. In small doses caffeine actually helps, but stop after the first cup of coffee. The law of diminishing returns kicks-in and blood flow to the brain actually begins to diminish. There's a lot of stuff we can do to enhance our brain function. A great resource for overall brain health is Dr. Daniel Amen's site (amenclinics.com). Take a look and find all kinds of ways you can optimize your noggin. And, a chocolate covered Oreo *once in a while* isn't so bad. There need to be *some* rewards.

Exercise. Yep, we know this one, too. Daily exercise increases blood flow to the brain. The better the flow, the better our brain works. The fringe benefit is 6-pack abs. Well, maybe.

Challenge. Challenge is the gymnasium for the brain. We need it just as much as we need to walk a treadmill or do 1,000 crunches every day. Solving problems gives us a focus for our energy. By working on problems in arenas that interest us, the more focus we give, the more energy we actually generate. I don't know exactly why this is true, but it is. I think it has something to do with the whole idea of flow. Flow is that sense of timelessness we experience when we work on something that fascinates us. Although there is a problem we're focused on, a positive stress - creative tension - is in evidence. This kind of tension is actually necessary to the process and acts as fuel to keep our engine running. Having enough energy is never in question. It's just there.

Work from strength. When we're forced to focus on stuff that doesn't interest us or is stressful, the opposite effect happens. Our energy gets siphoned. We become fatigued, exhausted. Our focus and attention wane or are stretched beyond our limits. Obviously there's stuff we have to do that we don't want to do. The trick is to reduce those to a minimum, and then focus on our strengths. When we work from our strengths we begin capturing that feeling of flow.

Challenge invigorates rather than exhausts. As we age we can't afford to *lose* energy. We need to find ways of consistently generating energy. Working from strength does that. This is an elixir that should help generate and sustain more energy. Hopefully it helps - especially all of you who know you can contribute more and make life after 40 more exciting, adventurous and meaningful.

Another powerful way you can manage and synthesize your energy is to do something extraordinary: *don't force an outcome!*

Forcing an outcome subverts the incubation process and you end up with something like *Plan 9 From Outer Space* (the worst movie ever made). Don't go there.

Instead, practice a little Zen. Let go of the outcome.

Outcomes

Outcomes, Results & Statistics: The Art of Zen Golf

"I have a tip that will take five strokes off anyone's game: It's called an eraser."
—-Arnold Palmer

It's a gorgeous early summer morning. The sunshine falls sweet and tender upon the first fairway, glimmering with promise. From the tee-box, the distant green is as smooth as fine crystal, and the fellows you're partnered with are in high spirits. After all, a day at the golf course is better than any 12 or 14 hour grind at the office, right?

Maybe. By the fourth hole you've already lost two Titlist Pro V's, you need a calculator to tally the number of shots you've taken, and you've become well acquainted with sand, water and weeds. The guys you're playing with have either become cutthroat competitors or they're secretly making fun of your backswing while you're at the tee.

In a 2002 survey of CEO golfers, Starwood Hotels and Resorts reported that 82% of executive golfers cheated, 85% were embarrassed by bad behavior on the course, and 26% had actually broken a club in frustration. Given that 87% of executives wagered on golf, these findings may not be surprising. After all, when money is at stake, outcomes count.

But, golf is supposed to be fun, isn't it? Played with character and restraint, right? Isn't that what Harvey Penick taught us?

Mark Twain called golf "A good walk spoiled." And, for so many golfers, he was right. After all, in the park-like settings of our best country clubs, one can hear a vast and diverse array of expletives. Obviously, it doesn't have to be like this.

Nearly 15 years ago I was one of those golfers. I'd picked up the game in my late 20's. Having been a pretty fair athlete who played college baseball and had remained in decent shape, I thought I could do pretty well at this strange game. I found out how wrong I was very early, but golf gets in your blood. It's hard to put away the sticks, even when you just hack.

Within a couple of years I consistently shot in the high-80's to mid-90's. The more I played the more pressure I put on myself to shoot better scores. While I didn't scream expletives or throw my bag into a pond after missing a 4-foot birdie putt, my stress levels increased while I became incredibly self-conscious during every swing. It just wasn't fun.

Then the reality brought me to a screaming halt when I suffered a full rupture of my right Achilles tendon. In a series of three casts for nearly four-months and unable to play golf for a year, I began re-evaluating just about everything.

One decision I made was to enjoy myself more on the golf course. When something of value is taken away, appreciation for what's suddenly gone rises exponentially. In my eventual return I decided to no longer keep score (a sacrilege, I know). And, long before Dr. Parent wrote *Zen Golf: Mastering the Mental Game*, I was playing Zen Golf.

My approach was simple. Treat every shot as an individual event. Empty my head of all thought. Breathe deep and slow. *Relax*. See the ball, hit the ball. Watch where the ball lands. Don't get attached to the outcome. *Don't keep score*. Enjoy the beauty and serenity of my surroundings (while shutting out the expletives coming from adjacent greens).

This led to an even more profound appreciation for the game, and, strangely enough, it had some wonderful side effects that spilled over into other areas of life. While at work I experienced deeper concentration and greater clarity. I relaxed more at home. My interpersonal relationships improved. I experienced less stress overall.

And, ironically, my golf game improved. After playing this way for a while, I had the intuitive sense that I was taking fewer and fewer strokes. While I didn't keep score, friends I'd play with would often comment on how my game had improved. When they asked what I'd done, I'd tell them about Zen golf.

Many laughed. Some thought I'd gone nuts. *"You don't keep score?"*

But, at the end of the round, when inevitably my score (according to their cards) was lower than theirs, they'd ask how they, too, could learn to play Zen golf.

"First, realize there is only one Arnold Palmer or Tiger Woods. We aren't them, and never will be like them. Just be yourself. Play your game.

"Second, I don't wager on golf. The game is interesting and challenging enough that I don't need to 'spice it up'.

"Third, I just want to relax and have fun. When I 'got' these three things I actually began to play better, though that's not my goal."

I suppose I was inspired by Ty Webb, the Chevy Chase character from the movie *Caddyshack*. Never attached to an outcome and, seemingly, simply out to have a good time, he hit amazing, once-in-a-lifetime shots on a continual basis. While I don't hit that many amazing shots, more often than not I'm satisfied by my play. And that's good enough. The best part is that I actually feel refreshed. The stress is gone. His philosophy? *"Be the ball."*

The course has become like a meditative sanctuary where the problems of business and the rest of life can disappear. And, carrying this relaxed state-of-being, my creativity, energy and clarity are all improved.

It's also helped with managing ADHD. The game requires frequent, but short, bursts of focus, with longer periods of mind-rest. I don't think about the game from shot-to-shot...I just walk and enjoy the beauty around me. It's refreshing, and it trains me to control my focus.

I consider that a pretty good trade-off from keeping score.

* * * * *

Exercise #11: What's your Zen spot?

The "Zen Spot" is that place you go to where outcomes don't matter. It is a place of mastery.

There's no pressure. No expectations. People don't clamor for you to produce. No bosses looking at their watch with furrowed brow. It's only you and what you love doing best.

When you're doing it, time stands still. It no longer matters. A kind of deep and abiding peace settles in, and you wish you could stay there forever.

To truly master your art you need to find this place and spend as much time there as possible. If there was one key environment you need to find, this is it. Search your soul. You know where this place is.

Get really quiet. Focus without thinking. Where does your heart lead? Is this your special place? Resolve here and now that you'll spend some time there every day - physically or in your imagination. Just get there.

And when you arrive, vow to not keep score. Just play.

Part III Summary

The creative process has many moving parts, but remains pretty simple. It's shaped like an hourglass. In the beginning we pluck a problem from the realm of chaos and systematically give it form. Once we give it form, we release it to the world.

That's it. But, like I said, there are many moving parts.

During this creative journey there is one absolute certainty – you will have to step off the cliff of comfort into the void of uncertainty. Yes, you will leave your comfort zone. But, armed with the 3-P technique (Planning, Practice, Patience) you can remove the edge. It also helps to have a supportive spouse or partner.

The Muse – she is flighty, but always around. Catch her and she will remain with you – so long as you are committed.

As someone with ADHD, you are an idea machine! Have a system for testing ideas and organizing them if an idea's time hasn't yet come. The Personal Slush Pile is an effective system.

What is the one thing that really drives your interest? Nail it down and focus on that one thing, never letting go.

Writer's write, painters paint, inventors invent. Quit talking about what you would like to do, just do it. And keep doing it!

The more you work on your one thing, the deeper your desire, and passion will build. Desire fuels energy – which is something you will need.

Focus your attention on the one thing – for those with ADHD, use the tool presented here to protect your focus.

After working a problem for a while and you hit a brick wall, walk away for a bit. Let it simmer and incubate. The answer you seek will come to you.

Quit keeping score – let go of outcomes during the process.

Part Four: Adversity

Wrestling with Angels (There Will Be Blood)

"If you're going through hell, keep going."
—-Winston Churchill

"Problems are the price you pay for progress."
—-Branch Rickey

"The most successful people are those who are good at Plan B.
---James Yorke (mathematician)

"The best way to kill creativity is to let the boss speak first."
---Victoria Holtz

"You win some, lose some, and wreck some."
---Dale Earnhardt

"There's nothing that cleanses the soul like getting the hell kicked out of you."
—-Woody Hayes

Wilderness

It's a Wild World

"Wilderness is not a luxury, but a necessity of the human spirit."
   —-Edward Abbey

"The creative is the place where no one else has ever been. You have to leave the city of your comfort and go into the wilderness of your intuition."
   —-Alan Alda

It really is a wilderness out there. And, *in there*.

We live in an age of monumental uncertainty. It seems like nothing is within anyone's control. The entire world - even with all our gadgets and collective knowledge - remains a wilderness.

The moment we step outside the comforts of our homes, we enter uncertainty. We may think we have control, but there is a vast unknown that's always peering over our shoulders. It wraps around us. The uncertain is always present.

For example, three years ago two women we know were diagnosed with pernicious and debilitating cancers growing through their bodies. Both were under the age of 50. Danielle, a devoted wife and a mother of two, died in early 2010. The other, Lori, battled daily, holding firm to her monumental will to live and trusting in her absolute faith in God's plan for her. He finally took her home in late 2011.

10 years ago most people had a job. Today nearly one in eight is unemployed, under-employed or have just given up. There are qualified people who have gone jobless for three years or more. One night I saw a news report that showed a smart looking man in a business suit standing on a street corner with a meticulous sign that read, *"Marketing Executive Seeking Work"*. Their worlds were once predictable. No more.

My friend's son served in Iraq. One moment he was with his platoon, riding in an armored Humvee. The next moment his vehicle exploded as it ran over an IED. He lost both of his legs.

It's a wilderness, alright. We don't know what's waiting around the next corner. It's an exploration and adventure every day.

But, I think the wilderness begins *within*. Both of the women diagnosed with cancer chose to see their diagnosis as just another leg of their journey. Neither gave in. Both utilized every gift God gave them, and every ounce of persistence and faith to fight and become well. Their journey into the gnarling teeth of the wilderness pushed them to creative lengths which they never thought possible. Danielle and Lori each believed they became stronger people.

"The Promised Land always lies on the other side of a wilderness"
 —Henry Ellis

In my business I see the creative lengths that people utilize to find and/or create meaningful work. Small business owners are re-examining their business, understanding they need to change. Their wilderness experience has caused them to remove barriers that had once held imagination in-check. One woman, the owner of a coffee house, has brought forward her grandmother's Cioppino recipe, bringing the 100-year old family recipe to market. Venturing into the unknown, her compass is guided by a lot of faith and a solid marketing plan.

My friend's son never looked back at his lost legs. Outfitted with special prosthetics that allow him to run, he's training for a marathon and has aspirations to become a police officer. While the wilderness took his legs, it didn't take his spirit. Or his imagination.

I'm grateful for the wilderness.

While uncertain and sometimes scary, it's a place of tremendous opportunity.

First, wilderness is a natural and necessary experience in which we are tested and forged. Were it not for the 40-years of wandering in the desert, Moses and the Israelites would not have been prepared for the thousands of years of challenges the Jewish people would face in the Promised Land. Had the Mountain Men of the early 1800's not ventured into the unknown wonders of the Rocky Mountains, the movement west would not have happened as early in U.S. history as it did.

Second, wilderness gives birth to our creative gifts, bringing them to the forefront. In the old days, when we were thrust into the density of the jungle or the arid wonder of the desert our physical survival depended on these creative instincts.

It is a different kind of survival, or evolution today. The wilderness has become more about shifting economies, politics, relationships and so many other elements of our modern life. When Eli Whitney invented the modern version of the cotton gin in 1793, he had no idea that his invention that made picking cotton cleaner, faster and more efficient would give rise to Konrad Zuse inventing the first freely programmable computer in 1936, and then the personal computer explosion kicked-off by Steve Wozniak's invention of the Apple I. The cyber-wilderness was given birth.

What does the wilderness mean to you? We just have to recognize that when entering the wilderness, we need to let loose the wild man or woman in each of us. That means, of course, giving our own internal wilderness the opportunity to be expressed every day.

Believe it or not, people with ADHD are naturally equipped to venture into wilderness. Let's face it, we've encountered adversity most of our lives. Granted, most of it was from stuff we created, but, nevertheless, for whatever reason, our brains were wired differently and that allows us to see divergent and multiple paths through the wilds.

We just have to trust these gifts.

What is your wilderness? Are you ready to embrace it?

Jacob was.

Wrestling with Angels

"So Jacob was left all alone, and a man wrestled with him till daybreak."
---Genesis 32:24

When Jacob encountered the Angel of the Lord, he was in the wilderness.

The wilderness is the unknown. It is a land filled with danger and opportunity. There is nowhere to hide, nowhere to retreat. To make it through the wilderness, one must move forward.

If ADHD is a blessing, and angels are those who often deliver blessings, then we will inevitably wrestle with angels.

ADHD, if left unmanaged, can be our biggest challenge. Without management, we face a multitude of issues that include:
    Relationship and marital issues;
    Disorganization and prioritization issues;
    Restlessness and chronic boredom;
    Anger, anxiety and low-self esteem;
    Distractibility and concentration issues;
    Procrastination, not completing tasks;
    Forgetfulness;
    Tardiness;
    Beginning tasks; and,
    Depression and other mental health issues.

Unmanaged ADHD isn't pretty. For anyone. It leads to a life commonly called "a train wreck".

Outsiders, "normies", look at our lives and stare in wonderment and shock: "How can they live like that?" "All this stuff is...preventable!"

Of course, they are right. Chaos - a principal characteristic of unmanaged ADHD (and even, at times, managed ADHD!) - can be controlled. When we manage our blessing, life - especially with regard to relationships - can be normalized to a large degree.

However, as one blessed with ADHD, I can tell you that it will never be "normal" - at least, not by conventional wisdom. And that's the point...people with ADHD tend not to have common sense. We have un-common sense. We see the world differently. And that's needed in this world of conformity and sameness.

But, we fight this. In order to get along, we want to be normal. And so, we wrestle with angels.

Throughout the Bible and other sacred texts, angels were often messen-gers. They would bring news from the divine, guidance from God, minis-ter to those who toiled on behalf of a holy mission. They would also bear warnings, bring tidings of joy, and would make other pronouncements on behalf of Heaven.

Angels direct man down paths that should be taken. As ADHDers, we often fight this direction. We want to be normal. We don't want to be dif-ferent. We battle the internal forces that drive us in our quest to fit in. However, the harder we try, quite often the worse it gets.

Or, we give absolute power to our internal forces. We fly by the seat of our pants, make impulsive decisions left and right, not giving thought to the consequences of these actions. We start new projects every day, never finishing any of them. We're left being under or unemployed, never reaching our potential; we constantly live in relationship hell - creating chaos for others (especially spouses and significant others); eventually we're mired in a kind of poverty that is difficult to break. It's all inclu-sive: emotional, economic, spiritual.

Both scenarios are the result of wrestling with angels. In these scenarios, we wrestle and eventually the angel (who could obliterate us with just a lift of the pinky) simply retreats. They leave us to our own devices.

But, Jacob didn't relent when he grappled with the angel.

I contend that Jacob fought angels for a long while. He did some pretty under-handed and despicable things. Through his impulsivity he entered into a contract with Laban without reading the fine print - and after seven years of toil he didn't get his reward, Rachel's hand. And so he worked another seven years. (It's been said that it takes people with ADHD twice as long as a "normal" person to complete work...strong evidence that ADHD was a part of Jacob's make-up).

Jacob wanted something from the angel. But, before granting his request, the angel tested Jacob's will - and his heart. The reason Jacob was on the road was that he was obedient to a vision given to him by God. The angel appears as a challenger, testing Jacob's resolve. Jacob's desire and commitment to his course are found righteous, and he is blessed.

There are rewards for wrestling with angels sometimes.

How can you tell the difference between a productive or unproductive battle? Here's the litmus test: if you are engaged in managing your ADHD, and you have a grasp of the process, angels (in the form of positive challenges) will appear to test your resolve. If you do not relent, they will bless you - though they may also extract a price from you (more on that later).

If you are not actively managing your ADHD, and you are haphazard in your approach, angels will come to re-direct you. If you fight them, they will relent without blessing you.

That is the difference.

And it is the difference between making it through the wilderness, or getting lost.

Cutting through the Creative Wilderness (no excuses, please).

"I don't like formal gardens. I like wild nature. It's just the wilderness instinct in me."
---Walt Disney

Aaron Gayden is a top-rate musician and composer. A while back we were talking about what it means to be creative, where it comes from, and how we sometimes fall into what's called "the creative wilderness".

For Aaron and so many others it can sometimes be caused by external factors. Things like working on a marriage, paying a mortgage and making sure our kids are okay and safe can put creative stuff on the back-burner. Unfortunately, sometimes it isn't enough to compose brilliant and beautiful music or string together words that connect with someone's heart. Sometimes one just has to pay the bills.

Real life can crash hard and fast into the golden halls of our creative dreams. Sometimes the Muse just isn't there – she wants us to clear the junk away. Occasionally personal dramas come into play (c'mon, we all have them). It's tough to concentrate when in the midst of relational fine-tuning with a friend, boss, children or your spouse. Sometimes, as Aaron and I have both experienced over the years, a new direction is in order but the compass isn't working. We're waiting for The Call.

The Call is a vital and sublime message that, when heard, supersedes all else except God, marriage and children. When it's heard and followed, life becomes turbocharged with purpose, passion and excellence. When it's not there, or it's languishing somewhere as a vague outline or an unintelligible murmur, life can be a dreary struggle. A spark of life is missing, making our experience of life incomplete.

What can we do when we're caught in the creative wilderness with a dull machete? Here are a few ideas that may bring The Call a little closer to home:

1. Keep working. Continue to write, compose, play music, market, sell, lead...whatever it is that you do to give expression to your creative spirit. The Call will *never* come if you stop working.

2. Avoid "Negaholics". You need positive influences. Avoid negative people at all costs. First, negativity can suppress creativity. Second, you become who you hang-out with. So, put the negative people on hold.

3. Reach out. Surround yourself with people you like and trust. Talk to other creative types. Seek help and guidance from others in your field, or from those in other creative fields. You'll find that all of us have been in the wilderness before...and there's a way out.

4. Read. No matter what field you're in, reading is a stimulus that kick starts the brain. Reading is interactive. It causes the imagination to work.

It also opens the receptors of your brain to receive important creative messages.

5. Let go of expectations. Many times we get stuck because we're holding onto outcomes. Let them go. When you do, you free yourself to create for creation's sake...and that's when you do your best work. When you do your best work, doors open. When doors open, The Call is typically on the other side.

6. Connect with God/your Higher Power. Prayer is a communication with something/somebody higher than yourself. It's an integral part of creating. To think that I am solely capable of creating something wonderful and fantastic is arrogance. To seek the assistance of something far greater than myself is not only wise, but ultimately productive.

7. Refuse to make excuses. When all is said and done, there is no excuse for not doing what you were Called to do. Excuses are the worst form of self-expression. Make a point of being dead-pan honest with yourself and, when you make an excuse, stop for a moment and call yourself on it. Also, be willing to listen to people whom you trust when they call you on your excuse-making.

A Calling is something greater than yourself. With God's help, you are entirely capable of hearing and following your unique Call, capable of creating your own Sistine Chapel or composing your own great symphony.

Quite often your next Big Idea is just on the other side of the Creative Wilderness. Keep this in mind while you're in it, and the trip through the jungle can actually become a blessing rather than a struggle. After all, the wilderness can be a magical place filled with unforeseen pleasures.

One thing you'll find is that most, if not all of the adversity you face, actually comes from you.

Resistance

Giving the devil some hell.

"If you wanna get to Heaven, you gotta raise a little hell."
——Ozark Mountain Daredevils

A lot of people don't believe in the devil. But, I do.

I see his scrawny ass every time I yield to Resistance.

In his excellent book, *The War of Art*, author Steven Pressfield says that Resistance is the chief culprit in zapping mankind's creative juice.

Resistance keeps you from sitting at the keyboard and writing.

Resistance keeps you from working out regularly in order to experience good health.

Resistance keeps you glued to the football game on TV when you could be spending time playing with your kids.

Resistance is what keeps you from making the call to the local expert you'd like to have as a mentor.

Resistance keeps you from getting where you really want to go - and keeps you exactly where you are.

Make sense? Think about this: The hardest part of being a salesman is getting out of your car or picking up your phone. Call reluctance (or, resistance) is what keeps average salesmen average. Breaking through the resistance is what makes a salesman great. It's all about energy in action.

Every one of us has our resistance points. You know, those guilty pleasures that keep us from doing our work. I'm not talking about hooky-playing stuff here - but excuses we use to keep from getting off our butts to get our work done.

And, when I say "our work", I don't necessarily mean what we're paid to do.

No, our work is that activity that makes our souls sing. It could be writing, painting, yachting, bowling, selling, leading, gardening, or cooking. By now, you know what I'm talking about.

Thoreau said that most men *"lead lives of quiet desperation."*

I think that's true. I can think of very few people who consistently do what they really love. Either they bog themselves down so much in their jobs that they have no time to cultivate their passion, or they're doing stuff other people have told them they *should* be doing, or they just sit on the couch and feel sorry for themselves.

I've known a number of people with ADHD who just never find their niche. Many have trouble holding down jobs, so they are just busy surviving. They end up in jobs that are beneath their talents and giftings, and they just never become who God meant for them to be. All too often they listen to bad advice and don't trust their own hearts.

I think the devil takes great pleasure in watching us lead these lives of quiet desperation, never quite fulfilling the divine Call placed upon us.

But, when we finally catch-up with the Muse and put her to work, bang home the first nails of that new addition to our homes; type the first paragraph; make the call; when we do overcome resistance, we kick the devil where it hurts.

We were made in the image of the *Creator*. As such, when we *create* we're taking back a little of what the serpent stole from us in the Garden. Like a child imitating his dad, when we create we imitate God.

Whether you believe in a literal devil or simply acknowledge that we all have our personal demons to overcome, creating is the equivalent of giving the devil a little hell. And it feels pretty good.

Adversity

Creativity Demands Adversity

"Adversity has the effect of eliciting talents, which, in prosperous circumstances, would have lain dormant."
—-Horace

Creative tension is the magic elixir that fuels the process.

I can't recall who said it but a quote I read a long time ago has stayed with me. *"When I stare at a blank piece of paper I suddenly realize how hard God's job was."*

That's the truth. And that's the point of adversity. Filling the page. Hopefully with something worth reading. Or, at least something that just needed to get put on paper so it gets out of one's head, whether it's read or not. Sometimes I write just to fend off boredom, writing just to write. No purpose. Just the connection with stringing words together.

Some paint just for the sake of painting - the feel of camel hair on clean canvas.

Others dance, sing, pick hot acoustic licks while lounging on the sofa. Sometimes it's just a way to fend off boredom - the mortal adversary of every person with ADHD.

Maybe it's just what we *do*. What we *must* do. It is air and water.

Purposeful creation keeps the world moving forward. And it happens at an exponential pace. We've had an explosion of invention during the past 100 years that's dwarfed all the preceding records of man. Instead of discovering foreign new shores, we've imagined new technologies, discovered new internal lands and the like. That's the challenge that's marked this age: newer, better, faster.

It's progressed from ensuring our physical survival, to capturing our relationship to beauty; from social criticism to stories about the complexities of inner yearning and change. From those early petroglyphs to the work of our most *avant garde* modernists, there was always something else that gnawed at the soul. Connection to the divine. The desire for illumination.

It's the ultimate adversity, isn't it?

Why are we here?

What is our purpose?

Why do we struggle to create? The world has been here for a long, long time – and we are just flashbulbs in eternity. A poof of dust in time.

Why go through the tumult of the creative process, the struggle to be seen and heard, the thirst to make a difference? What does it matter?

Because, unlike any other species on earth, we are wired to make that difference. And, yes, it is a splendid struggle sometimes. The point is this: creativity matters. It is what defines us as being human. It captures all of our senses, our emotions, our physicality. The act of creation is an imitation of the divine. It matters.

And so, because it does matter, we endure creative tension, which can be perplexing, painful and immensely worthwhile.

* * * * *

Angst, Stress & Creative Tension - The Breakfast of Champions

"I love the smell of napalm in the morning. It smells like victory."
—**Robert Duvall from** *Apocalypse Now*

Most people have this romantic vision of being a Creative Type.

When people ask me what I do for a living, and I tell them I'm a writer, responses are a variation of the same thing: "Oh, that must be exciting…" or "That must be so interesting…"

Well, it is interesting. I've become a quasi-expert in numerous subjects and I've met a lot of interesting people. But, what they don't know is that it's a hell of a lot of work. Earning a living laying words on paper is a constant challenge – not just the creative stuff, but the constant chase for clients, record keeping, billing and all the other administrative stuff I hate to do. In fact, I only write about 40% of the time. The other 60% is spent doing business stuff. For me, because I don't like doing the administrative stuff, there is tension. I'd much rather write a 10,000 word white paper in a week than take an afternoon to do quarterly taxes.

As with running any business there is a ton of stress, angst and tension. Add to that all the other elements of life like marriage, child rearing, paying bills and maybe having a little time and money left over to take a trip or two, and you've got the angst of life happening.

When it comes to simply the work, to be a Creative is to live in two worlds. The first is a beautiful world of imagination, invention and soul-fulfillment. The other is like Dante's *Inferno*, with different levels of stress and tension. They balance one another in the eternal quest for creation. One can't exist without the other. And it's something you'll just have to get accustomed to if you want to reach your creative potential.

The best way to handle the tension is simply to work. Much like physical activity can help dispel depression, working your art will exorcise the demons that want to hold you back. So, when you smell angst in the morning, know that you're on the verge of breakthrough. Just keep working.

* * * * *

Why God Gave Us the Blues

"Audiences like their blues singers to be miserable."
—-**Janis Joplin**

"I been in the blues all my life. I'm still deliverin' because I've got a long memory."
—-**Muddy Waters**

"I merely took the energy it takes to pout and wrote some blues."
—-**Duke Ellington**

"The blues - the sound of a sinner on revival day."
—-**William Christopher Handy**

"The blues tells a story. Every line of the blues has a meaning."
—-**John Lee Hooker**

Man can't create unless he knows how to weep.

That's why God gave us the Blues - to learn how to cry.

When you need to howl at the moon, do it.

Excuses

Creativity Killers

"You can always find a distraction if you're looking for one."
—-Tom Kite

"It is the nature of the artist to mind excessively what is said about him. Literature is strewn with the wreckage of men who have minded beyond reason the opinions of others."
---Virginia Woolf

Arguments with your spouse. Watching television. Bad bosses. Too much sugar. Too much booze. Too many drugs. Criticism. Not enough Jimi Hendrix.

The creativity killers are out there, lurking in the shadows, awaiting their chance to pounce. And, when they do, they won't let go. You must either give in or fight. There's no in-between.

You can live with self-doubt. Every Creative Type at some time or another thinks he can't do it. The unpardonable sin is to give in and stop, paying way too much attention to those voices. Whether they come from your spouse, jealous friends, well-intentioned parents - thank them for sharing, and get to work.

If you give them too much validity, the hand holding the knife to your heart belongs to only one person - your own. Don't murder your own dream. Believe this, you'll bleed far less while you're working than if you're on the couch watching Oprah.

Without even trying, there will be enough crap in your life that must be dealt with. Avoiding the responsibility you have to your art only makes it worse. While you and your boss may be in the throes of a civil war, a cease fire will eventually come. You can either hit the bar or hit the easel. The choice is yours.

So, the best remedy for any creativity killer is to defy death. Creation is life. So, create something, anything, and tell the devil to go to hell.

Owning Your (Personal) Brand

"Branding demands commitment; commitment to continual re-invention; striking chords with people to stir their emotions; and commitment to imagination. It's easy to be cynical about such things, much harder to be successful."
---Sir Richard Branson

Who owns your reputation?

It's not you.

Reputations are strange things because it changes from person to person, sometimes situation to situation. The fact is, *other people* own your reputation. For example, you might be a high-level, top-producing account executive who is known for outstanding service delivery. Let's say you have 10 Fortune 500 accounts. For whatever reason, circumstances occur - you forget an appointment, then miss a deadline, maybe deliver a defective product to one of those accounts. You end up losing that account.

Is your reputation good or bad with that company? It's probably not so hot. On the other hand, nothing adverse has ever happened with your other 9 accounts...so your reputation is good with them. Seems obvious, right? You might control the circumstances that can establish a reputation, but you really don't own it. The people you serve own your reputation.

Why is this important to know?

When it comes to your *Personal Brand*, reputation is pretty important. But it's not nearly as important as those internal characteristics that *drive* reputation. Integrity, character, reliability, creativity, honesty, passion, talent, vision. These are the kinds of traits that *drive* your reputation, but, in the end, you don't control how others view you. You never can, or ever will be able to control your reputation. So don't try.

The Personal Brand is built from within. Let passion drive your creative impulses, and then bring form to your vision through your talent. Just live it honestly. After all, reputation is an outcome (and what have we said about outcomes…?).

For the courageous account executive that lost the account, she'll go forth and be driven by the investment she's made in her Personal Brand, not her reputation.

Always remember that your Personal Brand is who you *are*. Who you *are* drives what you *do*. If you allow reputation to drive your brand, you will always be at the mercy of other people's opinions.

The only opinion that matters is yours. If you are following the path appointed to you, and you've sought wisdom from those you trust (e.g. your mentor), and you have the support of people who believe in you and love you – then why do the opinions of others matter at all?

They just don't.

Here's the thing – if you were to go to a party at which there were 100 people, 25 would like you, 25 would hate you, and 50 wouldn't give a damn. Are you going to spend all your bullets trying to please those who hate you? Or, are you going to re-load with people who like you?

The point of this is to get past what others think. Let's face it, as a committed Creative Type, you are going to be a target. People with small minds and petty jealousies are going to throw darts, daggers and gossip at you. Ignore them.

Just keep working. Remember, the best revenge is simply in being happy. People who criticize and find fault live very unhappy lives. Don't pay attention to them. You have bigger fish to fry.

And, as you move forward, you'll have other obstacles to clear, and many paths to blaze as you make your way through the creative wilderness.

Being in the Weeds

Time is so valuable. I don't need to tell anyone that. But, it is. And, the more I get in the weeds, the more valuable it becomes.

From time to time in my business I get overloaded. Either I take on too much at once, or projects seem to take on a very long life of their own.

Because of this propensity a favorite client has dubbed me "Last Minute Jim". I'll somehow get the job done right when it's needed. It's sort of like the writing equivalent of taking a bungee jump from a bridge 500 feet above a rugged ravine. It's a rush.

But, all things being equal, I'm really working harder at staying out of the weeds. The older I get, the less energy I have to write until 2am and get up at 5:30 or 6. It takes its toll. I need to remember I'm not 22 anymore.

Nevertheless, there are times when I sacrifice my sleep for the sake of getting the work out. We all do that sometimes, don't we? It's part of the price to be paid.

At some point you will be in the weeds, too. If you have ADHD it's inevitable. Work will pile up. Problems will occur. Something out of the blue will happen – a car accident, medical emergency, your favorite baseball team will lose 19 in a row. Stuff happens.

When overwhelm grows like weeds around you, the wilderness takes over, what will you do?

As an ADHDer we want to handle everything at once. Of course, that makes things worse. After all – and this is something EVERY person with ADHD must remember and commit to their hearts – the harder you try, the worse it gets.

That is the Gospel truth.

So, quit trying so hard. Relax. Step back. Observe the mess from afar. When in the weeds, evaluate and then prioritize.

Give each task a label: Important, Urgent, Unimportant, Not Urgent.

Get all the urgent stuff off your plate first, one thing at a time. Don't stop until it's all done. Next, focus on what's important. Get it done. If something urgent comes up, get it off the plate and return to the important stuff.

You'll find that just about everything you focus on will either be urgent or important. The stuff that's not important and/or not urgent will fall away. You may wonder how that stuff got put on your plate in the first place.

Oh yeah...it looked interesting...

The only stuff that sticks is either urgent or important. And pretty soon you will no longer be in the weeds, the path will clear, and the wilderness will make sense again.

However, even if it does make sense, the wilderness *is* a dangerous place. Sometimes there are snakes. And you get bitten.

Snake Bites in February

When it comes to certain things, some people are just "snake-bit".

You know, nothing goes right or as it should; or certain disaster will come crashing down if a particular course is taken (and all others who take that course do just fine).

Kind of like the Brooklyn Dodgers. They went 50+ years without a World Series win. It was just a given: the Yankees would beat them back across the bridge every time. The Dodgers were snake-bit.

At least until 1955 - when they pulled off the miraculous and beat their well manicured rivals from the Bronx. Of course, we won't even talk about the Chicago Cubs here…

February is like that for me. It just seems the month of Cupid and I don't mix. This streak of snake bites began in 2007 when my father passed away on February 15th. He was only 66. The next year our favorite dog, Paco, had to be put to sleep. In 2010 my 88 year old grandmother passed on to ride an endless carousel with Herb, her one true love.

I'm not superstitious. But, three significant deaths within a four year period, all in the month of February? Some stars are playing with Laughing Sam's dice here…

That being said, it's easy to let stuff mess with you and give you cause to make excuses. No matter what's going on, or what the trends are looking like, the way to avoid snake bites and creativity killers is to just keep working. When it's time to take a break, take a break (and don't think about those goofy stars).

Sometimes when the weeds become especially high and it's tough to see the snakes, laying low is a good idea. Lord knows that's what I've done on many occasions.

Even when lying low - which is a great time to incubate new ideas and revive internal combustion - continuing to work and rest is important. Equally important is to quit making excuses for the snake bite scars on your ankles.

Excuses don't work. They just keep you stuck. If you have ADHD, you have made your share of excuses. I know I have. Heck, having ADHD is a built-in excuse! However, it ultimately doesn't work. The more excuses you make, the less life works in your favor. The creative life is hard enough as it is…why make it worse by making excuses?

But, all things being equal, I'd be quite happy to skip February for the rest of my life.

Of course, that's an excuse. I'll just have to see February as a part of the jungle I don't like and sharpen my machete to an even cleaner edge.

Exercise #12: Owning It.

Culturally, we've really become good at excuse-making. Nothing is ever our fault. And, for us, ADHD makes the perfect excuse! I know I've used my *neurological/biological condition* as an excuse many, many times!

Sometimes our failure to do something is caused by our condition. That's a fact. However, once you've been enlightened about your responsibility to manage ADHD, it can never be used as an excuse. We are *always* responsible.

In fact, we are responsible for every aspect of our lives, good or bad. This is called *owning it*.

To reach our creative potential, *owning it* must become a part of who we are. What this means is giving up our excuses (which includes blaming others), accepting full responsibility, learn, and move forward.

Begin to notice how you respond to things that don't go quite right. Do you make excuses, however subtle? Do you place blame? Take notice.

Also, when things go right, do you accept the praise or credit? Or, do you defer it onto others (even when it rightly belongs to you)? Notice your responses.

Ask a few people you trust to be honest with you. Tell them to call you on your ownage or lack thereof.

Over time, begin changing your responses. Also, watch your impulsive responses! ADHD often disables our internal editor - so make sure you don't blurt out stuff that could come back to harm you. But, if you do, own it.

Keeping Quiet

Playing Your Cards Close to the Vest

"Loose lips sink ships."
—**Advice to GI's in World War II**

Have you ever been working on a project that just wouldn't let you go? When you're into it, you lose track of time, you're hyper-focused, consumed? And, when you're away from it the details of the project are always front and center in your mind?

It's hard not to let your enthusiasm show. Either you find yourself walking into walls because all you can see are the possibilities; and, despite the bloody nose caused by those darned walls, a smile worthy of a Crest commercial is plastered below your nose 24/7.

Friends and family constantly come to you and say, *"Are you alright? Can I have some of what you're taking?"*

You tell them it's the "creative high" - and now they want to hear all about it. However, as you hunker down to reveal the secret of your new-found joy, a quiet little voice whispers in your ear.

"If you tell them you'll be sorry...so shut up!"

But, you're so doggone excited that you can't help but share the joy. Having your friends and family share in your excitement and enthusiasm can only be a good thing...right? But, there's that voice saying, "*Choose wisely...*"

When it comes to that moment, you have three choices.

Choice #1: You give them just a little information, enough to whet an appetite of curiosity. Your answers are somewhat vague, providing very little detail, but giving a general overview. Some of the people you tell will say "Sounds great. Can't wait to see the finished product." Others will give you the old California Kiss response - you know, the fake little kiss and the lie "Oh, so happy to see you." Only, they say, "Oh...sounds wonderful." They smile and wish you well, but don't really mean it. Finally, some of the folk you tell will just say, "Whatever." and go on their way. You have mixed feelings about the response. Doubt creeps in. Maybe you'll complete the project, but, maybe you won't. After all, *"Leroy and Blanche don't seem too excited about it..."*

Choice #2: Give vivid detail with unyielding enthusiasm. Some will love what you're doing. Some will try and talk you out of proceeding, not wanting to see you fail or be disappointed (after all, you're so happy right now - why spoil it with failure?). Others will just say, "Whatever." With two out of the three responder groups, your expectations have come crashing to earth. Devastated, you shelve the project and find something safe to turn your attention toward.

But, let's say everyone you told responded with wild joy and enthusiasm, praising you, showering you with hosannas and rose petals. Their approval singing in your soul, you go back to work on the project and...the thrill is gone, baby. You've spilled the script and now the poisonous mixture of being attached to an outcome, the expectations of others, and the sudden need to deliver winning results zaps the joy from your soul and you're smack dab in the middle of a B.B. King song. You have at it for a while, but time drags, ideas sag and you've got nowhere to go. You shelve the project, feeling like an utter and complete failure as your promising project hits the slush pile.

Choice #3: Say nothing. Tell no one. Lie if you have to. When they ask why you're so happy, tell them you just heard a good joke, or your husband/wife/SO/friend called and you had a wonderful talk; or maybe you just tell them you don't know why you're so happy, but you are, and you just want to enjoy the feeling for a little while. Whatever. Don't let the cat out of the bag.

When I was younger I killed many a project by opening my mouth. The slush pile is filled with half-completed manuscripts, idea sketches and brilliant plans that went nowhere. All because I couldn't keep my mouth shut. ADHD can be a very destructive thing – we can have a tendency to blab on and on about stuff we're excited about…and then, nothing.

So, this is an immutable law that every Creative Type *must* respect:

When in the throes of a creative process, keep thy mouth firmly shut. Tell nothing.

Provide no details. Play your cards close to your vest.

Do this and the mystery, excitement and pure joy of the process will never be lost. Do this, and you just might make it to the next angst-producing part of the process. A little thing we like to call having your heart cut-out with a spoon.

"No."

Embracing Rejection

"I've been reading reviews of my stories for twenty-five years, and can't remember a single useful point in any of them, or the slightest good advice. The only reviewer who ever made an impression on me was Skabichevsky, who prophesied that I would die drunk in the bottom of a ditch."
—-Anton Chekhov

I'm kind of a sales profession junkie. I subscribe to a bunch of newsletters and blogs written by sales gurus like Jeffrey Gitomer. I was reading over an article on Jill Konrath's blog, *Selling to Big Companies*, that resonated with me - *"Embracing Rejection is Stupid."*

She was responding to an article she read in which the author contended that in sales "the results were in the rejections", and "The secret is for each salesperson to realize how much rejection is necessary for success." She didn't buy into that, and neither do I.

C'mon, who in their right mind likes rejection? Unless you've got a masochistic streak, no one likes it. Rejection hurts. Rejection steals a little of your soul. Rejection just flat out sucks. It's like your best girlfriend lightly kissing you on the cheek and saying "have a nice life." It's the Judas Kiss and it's not fun.

I like Konrath's take. *"In my opinion, a rejection is a failure. It's a sales call that did not result in a desirable outcome. If you want to get better at selling, it is imperative to analyze your failures to determine if a different approach could have yielded a better outcome."*

I've always subscribed to the notion of "failing forward". If something doesn't work just right, study the process, determine where the gap is, then do something different. It's easy to fall into routines and keep doing the same thing over and over again and expect different results (that's called insanity, ok?). So, taking the "fail-forward" approach can really be liberating.

Selling, like any other business function, is part art and part science. Obviously, there is a lot of rejection - perhaps more so than any other profession – except writing and the arts. In order to insulate our psyches and our soul from all this rejection, we've got to have a way to take something positive from the experience.

This is especially true for us Creative Types. After all, we can be a sensitive crew. Here are a few ways I've found that make rejection a little easier for me to handle. Maybe they'll help you, too.

Don't beat yourself up. A lot of gurus say *"Don't take it personally."* Well, let's be honest. It's really hard to *not* take rejection personally. I think it's more important to not be *self-condemning*. It's easy to say negative things about ourselves when we fail. Don't do it. Acknowledge the hurt you're feeling, but then move through the hurt and just say, "I'm going to learn from this".

Share your pain. One thing my Morning Thunder friends and I would do is share the rejection letters we'd received from crusty editors who didn't like our work. We'd acknowledge our disappointment. We'd make fun of the overall lack of intelligence these editors shared. And then we'd laugh about it. It worked.

Look at your process. Once you get through the emotional part, get to work. Look at the failure from every angle. What was the part (that was in your control) that you could have done better. For example, I use sales letters to generate leads for my business. If a letter falls flat, I try and look at it through the eyes of the reader. I'm often blind to what's missing or isn't landing right, so I've learned to ask my editor (my wife) for her input. Since she's usually right on target, I've learned to give her my sales material *before* I ever send it. That's failing forward.

Be willing to learn. Be coachable. I used to be a real butt-head when it came to receiving advice. I figured "hey, I'm the expert here, right?" Wrong. A big part of my failure was thinking my way was the only way. When I would take that arrogant attitude things would just go wrong. I finally wised-up. I received the help. I became obedient to the process and didn't question the good coaching I was getting. Guess what? The results became better. However…not all advice is good. Take the advice and coaching from people you trust – you trust them for a reason, right? If others give what you know to be lousy advice, nod, thank them for the input, and find the coaching from a reliable source.

Pretend it's a puzzle. Finally, make a game out of it. While rejection sucks, the process afterwards doesn't have to be painful. Finding what works is a puzzle. Your job as a Creative Type is to find the missing pieces.

Embracing rejection is stupid. Learning from it is smart.

Exercise #14: The Fail Forward Principle

Think about a time when you were told "No." Why did that happen? How did it make you feel? Did you feel like a big failure?

Write out the scenario:

What did you ask for? If you received a "yes", how would that have changed your life? How did "No" change your life?

Looking back, what could you have done differently to get a "Yes"?

Could you have prepared more? Was there advice you didn't take that could have helped in hindsight? Were the conditions right in seeking what you wanted – was the timing off?

Dissect this – why did they *really* say "no".

If you really have some guts, call that person who rejected your proposal and ask why they said "no". Tell them you are attempting to learn and you would appreciate their honest assessment and reasoning.

Commit what you've learned to paper. Study the results.

And then make adjustments.

Do this and you will minimize the number of scars you collect along the way.

Sacrifice

Jacob's Cost – There *will* be scars.

"All want knowledge, but comparatively few are willing to pay the price."
——Juvenal

"One has to pay dearly for immortality. One has to die several times while one is alive."
——Frederick Nietzschke

While perusing some old updates from a newsletter I subscribe to, I found a story by Steve Tobak (*The Corner Office* blog) about passion. In *Finding Your Passion Takes Faith and Sacrifice*, he quotes Steve Jobs.

Jobs gave up something of value to pursue a gnawing sense that he was meant for something else. Jobs quit college and teamed with Steve Wozniak to create the personal computer. I appreciated what Jobs said to graduates during a commencement address delivered at Stanford University in 2005.

"Your time is limited, so don't waste it living someone else's life. Don't let the noise of others' opinions drown out your own inner voice.

"You have to trust that the dots will somehow connect in your future. You have to trust in something – your gut, destiny, life, karma, whatever. This approach has never let me down, and it has made all the difference in my life.

"The only way to do great work is to love what you do. If you haven't found it yet, keep looking. Don't settle.

"Being the richest man in the cemetery doesn't matter to me. Going to bed at night saying we've done something wonderful, that's what matters to me."

Passion is fuel for commitment. And sometimes to fill our passion-tank we have to leave something of value behind. This sacrifice - be it love, money, position, power or even a pound of flesh - will leave a scar.

Go back to the beginning with Jacob.

He wrestled with the angel. He received his blessing, but paid for it through his flesh. That scar was instructive.

Many want the good things in life. We all want our particular blessings. But, what price are we willing to pay? Yes, there will be blood - and there will be scars.

In ancient times the scars warriors received in battle were testaments to their courage, skill and willingness to do whatever it took to be victorious. The scars were a way of saying, *"I have chosen this life and these scars are a small price to pay. Better to be scarred than die."*

I also think of the scars Christ wore when he returned to visit his disciples after his crucifixion and resurrection. His scars instructed *us* to bear our own crosses. There is surely a price to pay if one is to ascend from the comfort of mediocrity.

Faith and sacrifice. A life worth living leaves scars.

The scars are a journal of your trip, a legacy, the map of your story.

Great deeds can't be won without being tested.

There *will* be failure.

There will also be a life worthy of praise - even if the praise comes only from a chorus of angels that your ears alone can hear.

And often that's enough.

Exercise # 14: Living with the Scars

People with ADHD have plenty of scars. Our impulsive nature, lack of boundaries at times, and our lapses in self-control lead us into the bramble bushes along the road. We get scraped and cut - and the thorns leave scars.

As we lead our creative lives, we will take many risks, not all of which will work out. There will be small things that become irritations that we can shake off easily, like water off a duck's back. Then, there will be other instances - like losing an account or failing to sell a painting or getting a bad review - when it will feel like the world has come to an end.

It will hurt.

Don't minimize or magnify the hurt. Be with it. Own it. Don't be a victim to it, allowing it to immobilize you. But, also, don't shrug it off and bury it. Allow yourself to feel it.

And then learn from it.

When you're past the pain, do this as an exercise. As an addendum to your Individual Learning Plan, keep a risk/reward journal. Describe the risk-taking activity. Explain why you elected to take the risk and what the reward was that you sought. Describe the outcome. No matter whether you succeeded or not, describe the lessons you learned.

After a while you'll accumulate quite a few entries. Without judgment, compare those times in which you succeeded with those times in which you did not. What's the difference? Do you see patterns? Do you see redundancies (are you failing at the same types of things over and over?).

Before taking your next risk, compare your past results. Can you do something a little differently this time?

People with ADHD can sometimes have short memories. Keeping this kind of journal can help overcome some of the challenges - and avoid additional scars - caused by impulsivity.

Part IV Summary

No matter what we choose to do in life there will be adversity. The point here is that if you are traveling a path doing something meaningful to you, the adversity is worthwhile. You accept it as a part of the journey. After all, every hero on a quest will have to face a few trolls and a dragon or two.

The world of creativity includes a wilderness. There is no denying this. The wilderness is a part of our creative DNA. This uncharted land has dangers and opportunity, and you must enter it to reach the Promised Land that waits on the other side. And so, adversity is necessary to the creative process – and it exists within the wilderness.

As you slash away the vines to create a path, there are certain techniques you can use to make your way through the wilderness a little less difficult.

Adversity is necessary. Don't complain or make excuses. Adversity sharpens you and makes you stronger. Embrace it.

When you feel angst and stress, keep working. It's cathartic. Work also keeps any number of problems away. Just keep going.

Remember, God invented the blues to teach men how to cry. Howl at the moon occasionally. Then, get back to your work.

The two biggest creativity killers (besides bosses) are excuses and resistance. Don't make any, and don't give in. Push forward.

There are very few opinions that really matter: yours, your mentor's, other people you truly trust. Shrug off the rest.

When in the weeds, prioritize.

Cutting through the Creative Wilderness is like a holy mission. Avoid negaholics and excuses, keep working, move forward despite the circumstances.

When you are working on a project that brings you joy and excitement, don't share the details until you're done. Sharing your work too early can literally snuff-out your joy and enthusiasm.

Do not embrace rejection. Learn from it. Fail forward.

The creative journey *will* leave scars. Count them as a blessing for a life well lived.

Part Five: Completion

Coming Home

"Home is not where you live, but where they understand you."
—-Christian Morgenstern

"I looked at my hands to see if I was the same person. There was such a glory over everything. The sun came up like gold through the trees, and I felt like I was in Heaven."
—-Harriet Tubman

"If we are always arriving and departing, it is also true that we are eternally anchored. One's destination is never a place, but rather a new way of looking at things."
—-Henry Miller

Balance

It's Cheaper Than Therapy

"It was either therapy or die."
—-Mickey Rourke

"Yeah, it's nice to get paid for therapy rather than paying $240 an hour for it."
—-Ron Perlman (Actor)

Had an interesting conversation with a friend of mine not long ago. The central question: would Van Gogh have been *Van Gogh* if his mental illness issues had been resolved by therapy or meds?

My friend, a chiropractor who's just about ready to graduate from a Neuropathy Diplomate program, suggested that Van Gogh's unique perspective was fueled by his mental illness. His creativity, in essence, was his drug of choice in "medicating" his illness.

I can think of a laundry list of talented people whose groundbreaking work changed the world, yet whose lives were tormented. Cobain, Morrison and Belushi, to name a few. Brightly shining stars who experienced a personal supernova.

Of course, for every Van Gogh and Cobain, there are hundreds of others who didn't implode. But, do we really know? It seems to me that every Creative Type is a little different, especially the ones who've contributed significantly to the progression of their art. Do all Creative Types have some varying degree of dysfunction?

A psychiatrist I know told me that many of the Creatives he treats have a common malady, a pre-frontal cortex deficiency. The frontal lobes of their brains aren't getting enough dopamine, etc. The act of creation brings on a neuro-chemical head-rush that tames the beast. Of course, this is a most common neurological condition of ADHD.

So, I asked him, "Does therapy kill creativity?"

He didn't know. But, he said that it's possible that the creative outcome might be very different. Would Van Gogh be *Van Gogh*? Maybe not. I do know that having ADHD is not a curse. It is a blessing. Recent studies have demonstrated that people with ADHD have a propensity toward higher degrees of creativity. Yes, it is a blessing.

I'm not disparaging therapy. I know many people it's helped.

On the other hand, I know a lady who exercises incessantly. Every morning and afternoon I see her running. She says buying a good pair of running shoes is cheaper than therapy.

Maybe making art is, too.

A Lesson from the Samurai

"The man whose profession is arms should calm his mind and look into the depths of others. Doing so is the best of martial arts."
---Shiba Yoshimasa (1350-1410)

Remember the old Saturday Night Live skits that featured John Belushi as a Samurai warrior? He would be operating a dry cleaners, deli or florist shop...and use his *katana* sword to make pastrami on rye, or design a floral arrangement. Really funny stuff.

But, it was also based *somewhat* on reality.

Samurai warriors were the most well-trained, efficient killing machines on earth. Respected and revered, they killed with impunity. Look at them funny or not bow to the *nth* degree...they'd slice and dice you without breaking stride or giving a backward glance.

Samurai masters, and the emperors that ruled them, were very wise, though. They realized that they couldn't let loose the dogs of war and expect the subjects of their realms to be safe. The killing instinct had to be tempered. So, during peaceful times, samurai warriors were encouraged to have an art. And so, a great deal of the art made during medieval Japan was made by samurais. Many became renown poets, calligraphers and floral designers (yes, many Bushido masters really did arrange flowers!).

As Daidoji Yuzan, a samurai and military strategist from the 17th century, wrote in the *Budo Shoshinshu,* "Though Bushido naturally implies first of all the qualities of strength and forcefulness, to have this one side only developed is to be nothing but a rustic samurai of no great account...he should take up verse making or Teaism (mastering the tea ceremony)...for if he does not study he will not be able to understand the reason of things either past of present."

The Emperor knew that balance was important. They wanted warriors who understood the many ways of life. It was the difference between raising a class of sociopaths and a class of well-made warriors who could apply the lessons of a balanced life to the battlefield. It also taught them the actual value of life.

It shares a connection to a "classical" education, in which the purpose of education is to form a fully developed person who understands culture, language, literature, mathematics, arts and science.

Today, though, we live during an era of specialization. People can make more money if they specialize in something. For example, a computer programmer who writes code for video games will make a lot more coin than a run-of-the-mill code monkey who can do custom spreadsheets. But, I wonder if specialization has caused us to become more ignorant and intolerant as a culture? After all, look at the current political environment. There is no room for creative thinkers - just ideology.

And in business, why is it that corporate executives experience more stress than other people, and actually have a life expectancy that is 10 years shorter than average adults? Simple. There is no balance. One-trick pony's often end up lame...

So, for practical purposes, Creative Types need to have balance. You need to have an outlet that doesn't involve your creative pursuits. Like a samurai writing verse as he looks upon the majesty of Mt. Fuji, find a connection to something else. Maybe it's the outdoors - hiking, fishing, camping, sliding down a snowy mountainside on a freshly waxed board. Perhaps it's taking drives into the country and stopping at antique shops. Whatever it is, make a point of doing it often enough that it creates within you a balance.

If you don't, you can count on more stress and even burnout. And, for Creative Types, burnout is paramount to a kind of death.

Keeping the Fire Lit - Avoiding Burnout

I had to ask myself: what was I, a middle-aged, gray-bearded, straight-as-an-arrow dude doing standing in the crowd as The Flaming Lips entered the stage from, ahem, a gynecological wonder. (Yeah, it's a long way from Mt. Fuji)!

Um, don't ask. Let's just say they birthed their party in a most unusual fashion.

So, with confetti cannons blasting and great big balloons bouncing about the crowd, the band playing songs I'd never heard before, and the two college kids in front of me sparking a joint, I just gave in and enjoyed the show.

And, it was a good show. A multimedia miasma of guitars, video and bits of flying paper. But, the whole day was kind of like that.

I took my daughter and three of her friends to San Francisco attend the Treasure Island Music Festival. A day of 13 bands, artists, poets, side-show performers and many, *many* attendees either dressed in black or donning apparel they must have found in a Haight thrift. Thankfully, I wasn't the oldest guy there. Bob Mould, guitarist for 80's alternative pioneer Husker Du, and whose band was playing, was older than me.

And just as thankfully, I didn't embarrass my daughter by tagging along with her. Keeping in touch via text all day, she did her thing with her many friends who were in attendance, while I cruised the grounds seeking shelter from the cold, biting wind coming off the Bay.

There was no shelter, so I just took everything in. I witnessed Herbie Hatman have a cabbage sliced open on his chest with a rusty cleaver while he lay on a bed of nails. I talked to a writer who had set up an old typewriter on a card table and wrote poetry-on-demand for people willing to part with $5. I caught the Tommy Guerrero Band (very good...reminiscent of a classic San Francisco Summer of Love jam band). I also delighted in Bob Mould who, at 50+, continues to play hammerhead riffs with a passion. There was also a painter applying brilliant colors to canvas and selling his stock, while graffiti artists used spray cans to create Picasso-esque art on large sheets of plywood, hawking their work for $150+ a pop.

To be honest, I enjoyed the heck out of it. Taking my daughter to things like this keeps my fire lit. I get a chance to be young. I get to stay connected with my daughter's culture. It takes me out of my ordinary. And that's a good thing.

As Creative Types we need stuff like this. We need breaks from the mundane. We need grist for the mill. For grizzled veterans like me, we need stuff like this to keep our minds open and fresh.

* * * * *

Exercise #15: What's your fire-stoking plan?

Ever wonder why so many great rock stars died at an early age? Hendrix, Morrison, Joplin, Cobain. And, why so many writers were drunks, drug addicts and derelicts? I don't think any of them understood energy flow and brain chemistry.

No matter how much we love to do something, burnout can come a-callin'. As was listed in *Let the Power Flow*, there are a number of things you can do to keep your mind sharp, lungs free of gunk, and legs sturdy and strong.

What's your game-plan to fight off the burnout blues? Do you have a strategy for maintaining consistency no matter what? It's important to understand how your body works. Brain chemistry is extremely important to everyone, but especially Creative Types with ADHD.

What is your plan for keeping your fires stoked, even in the midst of challenge, diversion and the sometimes tedious stuff that comes with every task? Take some time to consider what you'll do for each of these areas:

Sleep, Rest & Relaxation

Diet (keeping your brain chemistry in-mind)

Exercise

Outside Challenges

Improving Your Strengths

Learning (an ILP, perhaps?)

Your Environment (places and people)

Vacations (yes, you need to get away sometimes)

If you have a plan, you can stave off burnout and all the stuff you have to do to overcome it. For example, maybe you need to go fishing at least once every month in order to relax.

With diet, maybe instead of downing a Big Gulp, you can ease your way into drinking water most of the day. You get the idea.

Think this through. Don't take it lightly. You need to have a plan.

Because, if you burn-out, you may never get to experience the Bigger Purpose in store for you and everyone you'll affect.

Nobility

A Bigger Purpose.

"Gratitude is the sign of a noble soul."
   —-Aesop

"Do noble things, not dream them all day long."
   —-Charles Kingsley

Our Calling is our noble purpose. With this in mind, who are we to determine whether or not this thing we're called to do should not be done?

This Calling is divine in nature.

And it's not about us.

It's about others.

There is a story about the leader of a large Christian missionary organization. It was Christmas, and he instructed his aide to send a telegram to every missionary around the world to offer them hope and encouragement in what may be the world's most difficult vocation. The leader wrote three or four sentences and sent his aide down to the Western Union office.

A little while later the aide came back saying that they didn't have enough money for all of the words in the message to be sent.

The leader edited his original message, cutting it in half, and sent the aide again to deliver the message.

Once again the aide returned. The message was still too long. The leader boiled the message down to one sentence...and the aide returned again - too long.

The leader thought for a moment and then wrote a single word to be sent.

It was the perfect word for missionaries - and I daresay, all of us.

"Others."

This word captures the noble purpose. As creators, we are assigned the task and responsibility of practicing our art to the best of our ability so that we might benefit the lives of others. There is no other way to describe it. True creativity will always yield a benefit for other people.

Their joy is our reward.

And, the Creator compensates us for doing work that benefits others.

It's that feeling of oneness with purpose, of having meaning connected to life. We cannot help but feel the exhilaration of joy. This is our Calling.

Others.

Creation is a celebration.

"My desire is to transcend cultural, generational and denominational boundaries through worship. All that matters to me is that there's a love for Jesus, and a desire to know his love more."
—-**LouAnn Lee**

Art and spirituality have been married to one another for centuries.

From early cave drawings to movies of today with the highest possible production value, man has always been led by an internal need to express his relationship with a higher power. Whatever the explanation for this compulsion - be it an evolution of self-knowledge or a seed implanted into our collective psyche by the Creator, it is undeniably there.

The Noble Purpose lives in each of us - to transcend creating as an exercise in self-glorification, and give glory to a power much bigger than ourselves.

My friend, LouAnn Lee, is someone whom I admire deeply. The worship leader for Celebration Community Fellowship in Auburn, CA, LouAnn is also a national recording artist with nine CD's to her credit. Combining traditional gospel influences with the buzz-saw riffs of Texas-blues, her ballads will bring tears of joy, and then be propelled into the aisles as her husband, world-class musician Cedric Lee, pops a bass-line that would give Stanley Clarke and Bootsy Collins a run for their money. Needless to say, a worship service led by LouAnn isn't what your grandmother hauled you to when you were a kid.

What I admire most about LouAnn, though, is that she is fully committed to a Noble Purpose. With her incredible talent, she could easily be a Top-10 star in the world of contemporary Christian music. While a number of her songs have received considerable air-play, fame isn't her gig.

Instead, she uses her talent solely to glorify God, to benefit the people who attend her church, and to assist other churches around the country to improve their worship services. What she brings to the local church is a commitment to celebration. "Remaining faithful to the local church is so important. That's where we learn to live, love and forgive." She says. "A local church is where you grow up."

Purpose over fame and fortune. I think this is the true mark of creative integrity. This doesn't mean one can't get rich creating (*of course you can*), but to do so at the expense of your purpose is a mighty price to pay. LouAnn is perhaps the best role model I know with respect to being faithful to a creative purpose. She's living proof that you can make great art, enjoy a happy and fulfilling life, while serving a purpose greater than oneself.

It is done...Can You Hear the Angels Singing?

There is a moment of complete silence as you put down the pen or the brush. You take a step back and inspect what you've just completed.

It is a perfect moment.

Weeks, months or years of work have just come to a conclusion.

It is done.

Perhaps a wave of joy is followed by sheer exhaustion. Energy drains from you like a break in a levee. You put the brush or pen down and seek the comfort of a favorite chair. Maybe you close your eyes. A work has been completed. You have fulfilled the Calling of your soul.

And there is pristine silence. As your mind goes blank, in a far off corner voices begin to emerge. You hear singing.

In the stillness of aftermath, you can hear the angels singing.

I believe that when you have completed a work that is a function of your Calling, God is quite pleased. And His gift to you is the voices of angels raised in a chorus - "Well done good and faithful servant."

Your task is complete. The Creator will take it from here.

Afterword

What now?

As a person with ADHD, completing something is one of the hardest things I must do.

My personal slush pile is overflowing. I have many, *many* incomplete manuscripts and other projects. I've learned to accept that this is okay - and, as you read earlier, there's a way to make your incomplete stuff useful for a long, long time. Nothing is ever done in vain.

But, there's something soul-satisfying about completion.

I remember when, at age 26, I completed the manuscript for the first novel I'd ever attempted. After typing *The End*, I wept.

If you have ADHD, completing is a big deal. Celebrate it. Give it significance. Even if your eyes alone will be the only ones to see your creation, you have accomplished something of note! Take justified pride in the fact that you finished what you started.

This makes a difference - this knowledge.

Because you must now make decisions. What is next for your project?

If it's artistic in nature, what will you do with it? Display it? Sell it? Hang it on your wall? Send it to a publisher? Audition for a part?

Business and personal projects tend to be part of a larger system - you create or innovate in conjunction with others. What's your next move? How do you implement?

Once you finish, take the next step in the process. Give it to the world.

And then?

Start the process again. Go to your slush pile. Pick a project that you might want to complete. Or, start something entirely new.

Whatever it is, you now have a structure and process. And you *know* you can get it done.

Want more creative Blaze? Check out Jim's Blog:

www.BlazingMind.com

More great information on ADHD, the creative process, living the creative life, and a lot more.

About Jim

Jim lives with his wife Debbie and their two dogs in Northern California.

In addition to writing books, he is a consultant, coach and nonprofit executive. He has served in a number of executive positions with private sector and nonprofit corporations. He also owned a communications company that specialized in serving the needs of executive coaches and business executives on a global basis.